CHARLES EDWARD HORN'S MEMOIRS OF HIS FATHER AND HIMSELF

D1103999

Charles Edward Horn's Memoirs of his Father and Himself

Edited by
Michael Kassler

ASHGATE

STR
The Society *for*
Theatre Research

© Michael Kassler 2003

All rights reserved. No part of this publication may be reproduced, stored in a retrieval system, or transmitted in any form or by any means, electronic, mechanical, photocopying, recording or otherwise without the prior permission of the publisher.

Michael Kassler has asserted his right under the Copyright, Designs and Patents Act, 1988, to be identified as Editor of this Work.

Co-published by

Ashgate Publishing Limited
Gower House
Croft Road
Aldershot
Hants GU11 3HR
England

Ashgate Publishing Company
Suite 420
101 Cherry Street
Burlington, VT 05401-4405
USA

Ashgate website: http://www.ashgate.com

The Society for Theatre Research
c/o The Theatre Museum
1E Tavistock Street
Covent Garden
London WC2E 7PA
England

The Society for Theatre Research website: www.str.org.uk

British Library Cataloguing in Publication Data
Horn, Charles E. (Charles Edward), 1786–1849
   Charles Edward Horn's memoirs of his father and himself
   1.Horn, Charles E. (Charles Edward), 1786–1849 2.Horn,
   Charles Frederick 3.Composers – Biography
   I. Title II.Kassler, Michael, 1941–
   780.9'2

Library of Congress Cataloging-in-Publication Data
Horn, Charles Edward, 1786–1849.
   Charles Edward Horn's memoirs of his father and himself / edited by Michael Kassler.
     p. cm.
   Includes bibliographical references and index.
   ISBN 0-7546-3174-5 (alk. paper)
     1. Horn, Charles Edward, 1786–1849. 2. Horn, Charles Frederick, 1762–1830. 3.
   Composers–Biography. 4. Musicians–Biography. I. Kassler, Michael, 1941– II. Title.

ML390.H775 2003
780'.92'2–dc21
[B]

2003042176

ISBN 0 7546 3174 5

Typeset in Times New Roman by Computer Music Company, Sydney, Australia.
Printed and bound in Great Britain by MPG Books Ltd, Bodmin, Cornwall

CONTENTS

Illustrations   vi

Preface   vii

Charles Edward Horn's Memoir of his Father   1

Charles Edward Horn's Memoir of Himself   9

Appendices:

1   Charles Frederick Horn's Letter to the Compiler
of the *Biographical Dictionary of Musicians* (1823)   73

2   Charles Edward Horn's Draft Sketch
of his own Career (1828)   77

3   Charles Edward Horn's Account of his Father
in a Draft Letter to William Ayrton (1830)   81

4   Charles Edward Horn's Draft Petition
to King William IV (*c*1830)   89

5   The Horn Family   91

6   Correspondence of the Horn Family   95

7   Chronology   111

Index of Persons Mentioned   121

ILLUSTRATIONS

Isaac Pocock's portrait of Charles Edward Horn
as The Seraskier in *The Siege of Belgrade*
(exhibited at the Royal Academy, 1817)
(by permission of the Royal Society of
Musicians of Great Britain)   *Frontispiece*

Extract of Charles Frederick Horn's 31 October 1823
letter to the compiler of the *Biographical*
Dictionary of Musicians
(by permission of the Department of Special   *between 22*
Collections, Glasgow University Library)   *and 23*

Charles Edward Horn as Beauchamp in *Rich and Poor*
(by permission of the Harry Ransom Humanities   *between 22*
Research Center, University of Texas at Austin)   *and 23*

Charles Edward Horn as Caspar in *Der Freischütz*
(by permission of the Harry Ransom Humanities   *between 22*
Research Center, University of Texas at Austin)   *and 23*

Playbill of benefit for Matilda Ray
in which Charles Edward Horn performed,
Theatre Royal, Cheltenham, 30 June 1810   *between 22*
(by courtesy of the Cheltenham Art Gallery   *and 23*
and Museum)

Matilda Horn as Rosalie Somers in *Town and Country*
(by permission of the Harry Ransom Humanities
Research Center, University of Texas at Austin)   *facing 54*

Extract of Charles Edward Horn's 10 December
18[24?] letter to Messrs Sainsbury and Co.
(by permission of Jamie and Michael Kassler)   *facing 55*

PREFACE

The autograph memoirs of the composer, singer and actor Charles Edward Horn (1786–1849), in the Nanki collection of the Yomiuri Nippon Symphony Orchestra, Tokyo, are edited and published here, for the first time, by kind permission of the orchestra. They comprise an account of Horn's father, the musician Charles Frederick Horn (1762–1830), up to the time of Charles Edward's birth, followed by Charles Edward's narrative of his own life to 1818. An epilogue describes events in 1827, when he made his first visit to America.

Four shorter documents make their first public appearance in Appendices 1 to 4. Charles Frederick Horn's 1823 autobiographical letter is printed by permission of the Department of Special Collections of the Glasgow University Library. Three drafts in the Nanki collection follow, in which Charles Edward gives further details of his family and career. The remaining appendices present genealogical trees of the Horn family, a description of their known extant correspondence and a chronology of significant events in their lives.

Notwithstanding the education reported in his memoir, Charles Edward never learned to write orthographically, grammatically or very legibly. In a few instances it is not clear what word he intended to set down. It has seemed best therefore not to publish a transcript of his original manuscripts with all their faults but to provide, instead, a correctly spelled text, properly divided into paragraphs and sentences. This should communicate the documents' meaning more clearly than would pages full of misspelled or crossed-out words, ill-formed sentences and frequent editorial interjections of '[sic]'. Words that I have inserted to clarify the sense of the text are enclosed in square brackets.

History of the Memoirs. Charles Edward Horn's memoir of his father appears from its content to have been composed in the early 1830s; the memoir of himself from about 1845 to 1848. Both memoirs and the documents printed in Appendices 2 to 4 are in a notebook which bears the bookplate of the English music administrator and collector, William Hayman Cummings (1831–1915). The notebook also contains drafts or copies of about 62 letters by Charles Edward Horn described in Appendix 6 as well as diary entries and financial accounts for some of his years in America.

This notebook was not included in the *Catalogue of the Famous Musical Library of Books, Manuscripts, Autograph Letters, Musical Scores, etc. the Property of the late W. H. Cummings, Mus. Doc.* sold at auction by Sotheby, Wilkinson & Hodge in London on 17 and 21–24 May 1917. It presumably belonged to the 'residue of some 400 choice pieces' from Cummings's collection that 'were purchased ultimately by Marquis [Yorisada] Tokugawa' (1892–1954), founder of Nanki Ongaku Bunko [Nanki Music Library] in Tokyo.[1] In the *Catalogue of the W. H. Cummings' Collection in the Nanki Music Library* published in Tokyo in 1925, the notebook is listed on page 57, amongst 'books which have no direct connection with music'.

After a time when its whereabouts were not known, the Nanki Music Library was acquired in 1967 by Mr Kyubei Ohki (1906–1996). In the *Catalogue of Rare Books and Notes* [i.e., music] in the Ohki Collection that was published in Tokyo in 1970, the notebook is numbered 'K–44' and is entered on page 57 amongst 'non-musical materials'. After Mr Ohki's death his collection passed to the Yomiuri Nippon Symphony Orchestra.

I do not know when, or from whom, Cummings obtained the notebook. Charles Edward Horn's entries in it extend to 2 August 1849, so it probably was amongst his effects when he died in Boston, Massachusetts on 21 October 1849. As the obituary of him published in London on 1 December 1849 seems to draw upon information that he had written in this notebook,[2] it may have been sent to his family in England soon after his death.[3]

---

[1] A[lec] Hyatt King, *Some British Collectors of Music*, Cambridge, 1963, p 72.

[2] C[harles] H[enry] Purday, 'Memoir of C. E. Horn', *The Critic of Books, Engravings, Music and Decorative Art*, n. s. v 8 no. 208 (1 December 1849) p 558–559.

[3] Horn's entries in the notebook indicate that he was in correspondence in June and July 1849 with his sister Louisa and his son Charles in London. Purday

Abbreviations. In notes that accompany all the texts, and in the last three appendices, 'CEH' refers to Charles Edward Horn and 'CFH' to his father. The abbreviation 'IGI' stands for the International Genealogical Index of the Church of Jesus Christ of Latter-day Saints, available on the Internet through the Church's http://www.familysearch.org Web site.

All dates are presented in this book in day/month/year format, i.e., the day precedes the month. The symbols '<' and '>' placed before a date signify 'before' and 'after', respectively.

The preparation of this book has coincided with efforts by Colin Gowing to determine the genealogy and achievements of his Horn family ancestors and with Peter Ray's investigations concerning the family of Matilda Ray, Charles Edward Horn's first wife. I am greatly indebted to both of them for uncovering many records that without their help I would have missed.

Michael Kassler
Northbridge, NSW Australia
July 2003

---

presumably could have asked them for information to write the obituary, as he had worked closely with Horn in London in 1847 (see 'Horn's Oratorio— *Daniel's Prediction*', *The Critic of Books, Engravings, Music and Decorative Art*, n. s. v 8 no. 209 (15 December 1849) p 584).

CHARLES EDWARD HORN'S
MEMOIR OF HIS FATHER

John Wolfgang Horn was born 1737 [and] married Sophia Dorothea Shenaman.[1] [They] resided in Nordhausen.[2] One of her brothers emigrated to America and lived near Falbush or Fahelbushen near New York.[3]

J. W. Horn and wife Sophia had four children: J. Christian or Christopher, Jane, Charles Frederick Ernest and Mary (Maria). Charles F. was born in Nordhausen Feb 24th 1762 [and] emigrated to England after having been educated for a surveyor,[4] but [he] learnt and practised music unknown to his father, who often destroyed his son's clavichord that he might not neglect his study in that profession marked out for his future livelihood, but which had not the effect of discouraging him from his favourite amusement. One King or [blank] was his instructor, who was an organist and musician of high reputation in the town [where] they lived.[5]

These circumstances determined his leaving Nordhausen, and Paris was the city he determined to make known his musical ability in. And, setting off with a few dollars[6] and a small box of wearing

---

[1] In a note on another page of his manuscript memoir, CEH wrote 'Sophia D. Shenaman was the second daughter of Her[r] von Zinge—was born 1735'. The spelling of 'Shenaman' is not clear.

[2] The Stadtarchiv Nordhausen advise that Nordhausen baptismal and marriage records from this period have not survived.

[3] CEH may be referring to the Flatbush section of the New York City borough of Brooklyn.

[4] No evidence has been found to support the presumption of prior commentators that CFH's first name was spelt 'Karl' in Germany rather than 'Carl'. CFH consistently called himself 'Charles Frederick Horn' in England.

[5] In CEH's draft letter to William Ayrton, printed in Appendix 3 below, CFH's instructor is identified as the Nordhausen organist [Christoph Gottlieb] Schröter, 1699–1782. The name 'King' presumably is a mistake.

[6] i.e., German *thalers*.

apparel, [he] made for Hamburg. He there encountered a man he knew nothing of but, [this man] being an experienced traveller, he soon learnt the profession and destination of his young companion, an inexperienced traveller. This man's name was Winkelman, and whose winks turned out in one respect better than a nod in others; the sequel will explain. He advised the young musician not to think of Paris—they knew nothing of the piano, all played the fiddle there. But London was the true encourager of German talent. Besides, the Queen was a German woman, and this appeared to direct the young musician's attention. At length, as Winkelman was going also to England, the prospect appeared to be fairer. Besides, he had a companion, and one too that might do the musician some good.

A berth [for] each was secured in a London packet at Hamburg. And, upon arriving in London, the adviser and patron had no money, and the musician only enough to pay for both passengers. The musician began to reflect and, fearing his trunk might go too, he requested the captain to allow his trunk to remain on board a day or two. By that time he would make up his mind either to remain in London or return to Hamburg, in which case the trunk was to remain on board as hostage for his passage back to Hamburg, where he had friends, as he had scarcely enough left for two days' provision in a strange city. Accordingly, the patron Winkelman, as soon as the passengers were cleared at London Bridge and safe on shore, was missing and the musician [was] left with only 2 dollars and his great coat over his arm, without knowing a human being[7] or a word of the English language. However, being in no way discouraged, he thought he would walk till he saw a music shop, where probably there might be a countryman.

In Cheapside he found himself, and a music shop, then Broderip's, now Collard and Collard.[8] He walked in, sat down to a

---

[7] Therefore CFH did not know, and presumably was not related to, the musician Ferdinand Horn, who was active in England from the 1770s to the 1790s.

[8] A succession of firms that published and sold music and manufactured musical instruments were located at 26 Cheapside. From 1776 to 1798 these premises were occupied by the partners John Longman and Francis Fane Broderip; they were followed by Longman, Clementi & Co. until about 1801; then Muzio

piano and began to extemporise. This attracted the attention of a man cleaning the shop for, it [being] only about 7 o'clock [in the morning], the shop man thought it was some person known to the house, and the musician contented himself by playing on. However, nobody coming, nor any person speaking German, he walked out and then began to despair. St Paul's [Cathedral] attracted some attention, but not so much as to regain his confidence or brighten his prospect. The streets began to be crowded, even at that time, and the musician [continued] to walk on, knocked from one side to another. Temple Bar was an object of curiosity,[9] and St Dunstan's Clock,[10] being struck by two figures.

So that, while looking at this curiosity of wonders like the Irishman, a German fell against him, and swore in German. This was a short thick-set black-haired active man, bustling into the City. The musician seized hold of him, and the little German, being of a good-natured and kindly disposition, listened to his story [and] said it was a pity he should return. He should like to hear him play, and they walked on together till, arriving again at the same music shop, the performer sat down. The little German was delighted, and Mr Broderip made his appearance.[11] [He] was known to the German and both held a conversation in English [about] what should be done. The German was Charles Bertram, a music merchant, and a considerable amateur on the violoncello.[12] He had heard the butler of the Marquis

---

Clementi with various different associates operated there until 1831; the business then became Collard & Collard, who were there to 1834. Therefore this memoir presumably was written between 1831 and 1834. See Charles Humphries and William C. Smith, *Music Publishing in the British Isles from the Earliest Times to the Middle of the Nineteenth Century*, 2nd ed., Oxford, 1970.

[9] Located at the entrance from the Strand to Fleet Street in the City of London. In earlier years the heads of executed prisoners were displayed there.

[10] In Fleet Street.

[11] Francis Fane Broderip, music publisher, d1807, at that time in partnership with John Longman.

[12] In an undated c1830 draft letter in the Nanki collection volume, CEH mentions his plan to spend that evening at 'Mr Bertram's music merchant Bond Street'. Perhaps CEH meant, on both occasions, to write 'musical merchant' rather than 'music merchant', as 'Ch. Bertram & Son' is entered as wine and

of Stafford[13] say that the Marchioness[14] was endeavouring to find a pianoforte teacher who was capable of giving instruction or [and] would go to Trentham, their country seat in Staffordshire.

Bertram thought of this, but how they could recommend a young unknown? Broderip and Bertram consulted and questioned the musician how he could give any account of himself that would be satisfactory, provided [that] such an introduction could be got. This was referred to the captain of the vessel, and who was to have letters back to Nordhausen as to the fate of the emigrater. Bertram went to the ship [and] found everything so satisfactory that it was agreed upon to go that evening to Whitehall[15] and get an audience of the butler and the marchioness.

This all succeeded admirably. The Ladies Gower[16] were in Staffordshire. The Marchioness was going the next day, and the

---

brandy merchants at 162 New Bond Street in *Kent's Original London Directory, 1817* (London, 1817), *Kent's Original London Directory, 1828* (London, 1828), and *Robson's London Directory* (London, 1833), and no music merchant surnamed Bertram has been identified as working in London in these years. Both *Bailey's British Directory* (London, 1785) and *Wakefield's Merchant and Tradesman's General Directory* (London, 1790) include Charles Bertram as a grocer and confectioner at 7 Woodstock Street, and *Holden's Triennial Directory for 1805–1807* (London, 1805) lists Charles Bertram as a wine merchant at 5 Duke Street, St James's. A wine merchant named 'Carl A. Bertram', presumably the same man, was admitted on 27 March 1793 to the Pilgerloge, the German-speaking Masonic lodge in London (see the 'Hundertjährige Mitgleider-Liste der Pilgerloge' in *Festgabe für die erste Säcular-Feier der ger. u. voll. St. Joh.-Loge 'Der Pilger' No. 238*, London, 1879). No evidence has been found to connect Bertram the wine-merchant with the Charles Bertram of York House, Piccadilly, who is entered as a horn player in J[oseph] Doane, *A Musical Directory for the Year 1794*, London, c1794.

[13] Granville Leveson-Gower (1721–1803), 2nd Earl Gower, was created 1st Marquis of Stafford on 1 March 1786. Therefore he was not a marquis (and his wife was not a marchioness) at this time.

[14] Susanna Stewart (1743–1805), who had married Granville Leveson-Gower on 25 May 1768.

[15] i.e., to the London residence of the Earl and Countess Gower.

[16] Granville Leveson-Gower's two youngest children, Georgiana Augusta Leveson-Gower (1769–1806), who married in 1797, and Charlotte Sophia Leveson-Gower (1771–1854), who married Henry Charles Somerset, 6th Duke of Beaufort in 1791. Margaret Caroline Leveson-Gower (1753–1824), Earl

musician was informed what his salary was to be for 3 months, and that the Marquis was going down in three or four days' post, and that room should be kept for the young German stranger who, by the bye, it would not be improper for me to say as his son, for I have heard it often, that my father was a very delicate, fair and gentleman-like young man.

The day or two soon passed over and, one morning at 8 o'clock, the Marquis, a sturdy farmer-like looking gentleman and the young German musician got into a post travelling chariot at Whitehall, the present family's [London] residence, intended for Trentham Hall in Staffordshire.

Few words were spoken, and that only in English. At length the farmer-looking man ventured a few words in very bad German which was gladly answered by my father, and most respectfully too, for he had been informed of the rank of the family he was engaged in.[17] But he had no idea that it was the celebrated Lord North, then in office and a very powerful person in the government.[18] However, my father so began to find he was in most amiable and kind society, for Lord North made him understand he was anxious to practise his German.

Therefore, by this means, they instructed each other in German and English. A few days' sojourn introduced him to a young lady engaged as companion and French governess to the young Ladies Gower, an English young lady by the bye educated at the Ursuline convent at Boulogne in France. Her father was an English gentleman of French parents whose name was John Arboneau Dupont. He married an English lady of the name of Elizabeth Page from

---

Gower's eldest child (with his first wife), was then no longer living in her father's home, as she had married Frederick Howard, 5th Earl of Carlisle in 1770.

[17] On 19 December 1783 Leveson-Gower was appointed, for the second time, Lord President of the Council, and on 21 November 1784 he was appointed, for the second time, Lord Privy Seal.

[18] Frederick North, 1732–1792, 2nd Earl of Guilford, prime minister from 1770 to 1782.

Woodstock,[19] and the fruits of that marriage were John, Frederick[20] and this said young lady Diana Dupont.[21]

Charles F. Horn, the young German musician, soon found favour in the eyes of Diana Dupont. His engagement at the Trentham Hall was extended from 3 months to a whole year, at the end of which the music instructor and the companion of the Ladies Gower made a match of it.[22]

His conduct and fame soon spread in London. Christian Bach, the son of the immortal Sebastian Bach, retired and returned to Germany as instructor of the pianoforte to Queen Charlotte.[23] And Clementi had been appointed, [but] a circumstance concerning his family (Clementi's) obliged him to visit Italy.[24] And Charles F. Horn, at the suggestion of John Peter Salomon, the great violin performer,[25] applied for the situation. And, backed by the Marquis of Stafford, his family, and Lord North, who was then the patron and friend of

---

[19] On 19 March 1763 (IGI).

[20] Frederick John Dupont was christened on 17 June 1765 at St James's, Westminster (IGI, where his surname mistakenly is given as 'Arboneau' and his father's name as John Dupont Arboneau).

[21] Diana Dupont (1764–1831) was born on 4 March 1764 and baptised on 8 March 1764 at St Mary's, St Marylebone, London. I am grateful to Colin Gowing for securing a copy of her baptismal register entry.

[22] CFH married Diana Arboneau Dupont at Trentham, Staffordshire, on 28 September 1785. Therefore CFH presumably served at Trentham for about three years.

[23] CEH's statement is not true: John Christian Bach (composer, 1735–1782) died unexpectedly in London on 1 January 1782. See Charles Sanford Terry, *John Christian Bach*, 2nd ed., London, 1967, p 166.

[24] Muzio Clementi (composer, piano manufacturer, and music publisher, 1752–1832) appears to have returned to Rome, his native city, about the time of his mother's death there on 11 February 1785. See Leon Plantinga, *Clementi: His Life and Music*, London, 1977, p 73–74. No confirmation of CEH's assertion that Clementi received or was offered such an appointment has been found.

[25] John Peter *or* Johann Peter Salomon, violinist and concert promoter, 1745–1815.

William Pitt, Prime Minister of England at the early age of 23,[26] he, C. F. Horn, was appointed instructor to the Royal Family, [to] the princes[ses] of George the Third and Queen Charlotte.[27]

The young married pair, Charles F. Horn and Diana, his wife, now had left Whitehall, and took apartments in St Martins Street, Leicester Fields, then so called.[28]

---

[26] William Pitt, 1759–1806, prime minister from 1783 to 1801.

[27] Apparently this occurred in 1789. See note 10 on page 10 below.

[28] This memoir contradicts Charlotte Papendiek's statements about CFH's introduction to Earl Gower and the Horns' place in his household: 'The Marquis of Stafford, while travelling in Germany, met with this Horn, and, engaging him as his valet, brought him to England. He then married the housemaid' (Mrs Vernon Delves Broughton, *Court and Private Life in the Time of Queen Charlotte, being the Journals of Mrs Papendiek* ..., London, 1887, v 1 p 255). Charlotte Papendiek clearly disliked Diana Horn ('his wife remained just what she was, but Horn was of a good disposition, and by no means a low or vulgar man', *ibid.*, v 1 p 256), but her assertion that Diana's 'situation [i.e., pregnancy] soon caused my Lord to dismiss the pair' (v 1 p 255) should not be assumed to imply that the Leveson-Gowers were dissatisfied with their services. On the contrary, CFH's first publication, *Six Sonatas for the Piano Forte, or Harpsichord with an Accompanyment for a Violin, & Violoncello*, op. 1, entered at Stationers' Hall on 29 May 1786 after CFH had removed from Trentham Hall to 12 St Martins Street, Leicester Fields, was 'composed and most respectfully dedicated' to Lady Charlotte Leveson-Gower, who subscribed to it together with her mother.

CHARLES EDWARD HORN'S
MEMOIR OF HIMSELF

1786

Born 21st of June in the Parish of St Martins London and at N°
12 St Martins Street Leicester Square. Removed to Vauxhall. I was
put out to nurse at the end of this year in consequence of a probability
that a brother or sister was to make their appearance—when the
people who had the care of me let me fall and broke my left arm.[1]

1787

My brother Frederick Thomas was born.[2]

And I was christened.[3] Mr Edward Stephenson the banker of
Lombard Street[4] [and] Mr John Peter Salomon became Sponsors or
Gott Fathers. But Salomon coming too late, my father stood for him
in consequence. He always said he was never my godfather as I have
not been christened John Peter, although it was understood that I was
to receive the first name of my father and the second of Mr
Stephenson.

---

[1] CEH's assertion that his family removed to Vauxhall has not been
corroborated and may be mistaken.

[2] According to the IGI, CEH's brother Frederick Thomas Horn was baptised on
2 November 1787 at St Mary's, Marylebone Road, indicating that CFH and his
family had removed from 12 St Martins Street into that parish before then.

[3] CEH in fact was baptised at St Martin-in-the-Fields, Westminster, on 15 July
1786. I am grateful to the City of Westminster Archives Centre for supplying a
copy of the record of his baptism.

[4] 1759–1833, director of the variously styled banking firm Remington & Co. of
69 Lombard Street and musical amateur. Stephenson's subsequent involvement
in efforts to introduce J. S. Bach's music into England is recounted in my
chapter 'The English translations of Forkel's *Life* of Bach' in Michael Kassler
(ed.), *The English Bach Awakening: Knowledge of J. S. Bach and his Music in
England, 1750–1830*, Aldershot, 2004, forthcoming.

1788 to 1792[5]

My father was appointed about this time Instructor in Music to the Royal Family—having five Royal pupils to attend: the Princess Royal,[6] Princess Augusta,[7] Princess Elizabeth,[8] Princess Mary[9] and Princess Amelia.[10] This circumstance induced him to take a house at Windsor with his family.[11] Living there, I was, at the age of six years old, put under a Mr Page, one of the choristers at the Chapel Royal, to learn my notes and to commence the pianoforte.[12] However, he was an irritable and passionate man, and would fold up the steel strings of the pianoforte into a small stick about 7 or 8 inches long, with which

---

[5] CEH mistakenly wrote '1892'.

[6] Princess Charlotte, 1766–1828.

[7] 1768–1840.

[8] 1770–1840.

[9] 1776–1857.

[10] 1783–1810. The sixth princess, Sophia, 1777–1848, apparently was not a pupil of CFH. Queen Charlotte's Treasurer's Account shows that CFH was music master to TRH The Princesses from 29 June 1789, for which he was paid £200 per year plus disbursements for expenses. I am grateful to Miss Allison Derrett, Assistant Registrar, the Royal Archives, Windsor Castle, for this information.

[11] In Dean's Yard, Windsor, according to Charlotte Papendiek, who lived in a neighbouring house. In her journal, she recorded (see Broughton, *Court and Private Life in the Time of Queen Charlotte, op. cit.*, v 2 p 264) that CFH rented his Windsor home from a Mr Delavaux (perhaps Francis Hugh Adean Delavaux, whose son was baptised on 26 June 1780 at St George's Chapel, Windsor; see Edmund H. Fellowes and Elisabeth R. Poyser (eds.), *The Baptism, Marriage and Burial Registers of St George's Chapel, Windsor*, Windsor, 1957, p 31, and IGI). Mrs Papendiek added that CFH lived in that home with 'two or more sons [i.e., CEH and Frederick Thomas Horn] and one daughter' [i.e., CEH's sister Henrietta Elizabeth Horn, who was baptised on 1 April 1789 at St Mary's, Marylebone Road] as well as with 'his wife's German mother and sister'. The latter statement apparently is a mistaken reference to CFH's mother Sophia Dorothea Horn (1735–1798) and her sister, probably Mary Horn. Unlike Diana Horn's mother, they were German and did live with CFH and his family in London; see page 19 below.

[12] Rev. John Page, musician and editor, *c*1760–1812. He served as a lay clerk of St George's Chapel, Windsor, from December 1790 to November 1795.

he over an[d] over tickled my fingers till they bled, which so frighted and disquieted me with music that I dreaded a pianoforte as much as I did him. My mother remonstrated with him, but I was called an obstinate and stupid child: I could never learn music. And Mr Page's lessons were dispensed with, and the piano was shut up.

However, a year afterwards, I opened the instrument on my own accord and, being very fond of a French song *Ah! vous dirai-je maman*,[13] a song my mother used to sing and the only song I ever heard her sing, being one she learnt when at school at the Ursuline convent at Boulogne. I took such a fancy to the air that I not only picked it out by ear but made a bass to it. This so encouraged me that I resolved on composing variations to it, as I had heard talk of such things. And this said first variation consisted of a playing every note twice where it was wanted once, and when twice I repeated it four times—which sounded so very brilliant that I was continually at it when my father was in London, but never when at Windsor, for I feared Mr Page's assistance would be called in.

However, one summer afternoon I was rehearsing my variations when my father's return to London unexpectedly brought him to the door accompanied by Fisher, the celebrated oboe player who was in the King's band,[14] and the very same person who composed the *Minuetto* called 'Fisher's minuet' and danced by the royal family [and] all the celebrated dancers of that day.[15] This event determined my becoming a musician and, having got my mother to tell Mr Page's mode of teaching the piano, I was left to my own manner, although I could not learn a note by name yet [or] play many easy pieces by recollecting the notes on the lines answering notes on the pianoforte.

---

[13] This song has the same tune as 'Twinkle, twinkle little star'.

[14] Johann (or John) Christian Fischer, oboist and composer, 1733–1800, from 1780 chamber musician to Queen Charlotte.

[15] Fischer's minuet was famous in its day: according to Michael Kelly (tenor and actor, *c*1762–1826), it was 'all the rage' in Dublin about 1770 (see Michael Kelly, *Reminiscences*, ed. Roger Fiske, London, 1975, p 4). Mozart composed 12 variations on this minuet for keyboard (K. 179).

About this time I was taken to London by my father and left with an aunt. My father took it in his head to have boys' clothes put on me. Taking me down to Windsor on one of his trips in attending at the Lodge, a large party taking place at Mr [John] Ramsbottom's, the celebrated brewer, father of the Member of Parliament,[16] I was sent into the room dancing, where my mother was among the party but did not know me. Although I remember her scream!!! of delight at recognizing me in a nankeen[17] dress and blue sash. I can remember even now, 1845, the young ladies sitting me on the pianoforte and smothering me with kisses. Then came the trial of my musical abilities and the Variations were performed with considerable applause—and a hearty laugh from the musical party who were there.

My father made his appearance some half-hour afterwards, and I soon fell asleep, which I had done once or twice before in the post chaise. We had travelled in from town[18] when my father contrived to keep me awake by telling me we had come to the turnpike, which setting me into a fit of energy and almost hysterics, as I imagined, at that time of life, a turnpike was an animal in [the] shape of a small bear—such are the ideas of children.

About this time I was sent to [a] school kept by an old lady near the Cloisters, Windsor Castle and, what with going backwards and forwards from Windsor to 72 Upper Norton Street, London, I remember nothing but an old French manservant of my father's, who was very fond of me once, [and] always took me out fishing with him at Windsor and in London. [I] remember [him] by his carrying me from my own bed among my two brothers on a dreadful stormy night of thunder and lightning in the middle of winter. I now feel the cold

---

[16] John Ramsbottom Jr (*c*1780–1845) was M.P. for Windsor from 1810 until his death. Mrs Papendiek described his father, John Ramsbottom Sr, as 'the Queen's ale brewer' and a radical (Broughton, *Court and Private Life*, *op. cit.*, v 2 p 221). The Richard Ramsbottom, Esq., who subscribed to CFH's *Six Sonatas for the Piano Forte*, op. 1, entered at Stationers' Hall on 29 May 1786, presumably was the brewer's brother (*c*1749–1813), who served as M.P. for Windsor from 1806 until 1810, when his nephew succeeded him.

[17] A yellow cotton cloth, originally from Nanjing, China.

[18] i.e., from London.

in going through the landing place at the top of the house in the old Frenchman's arms, although I could not have been but 4 or 5 years old.

Time went on, till we lived in Lambeth N° 4 Pratt Street, a house my father took of Edward Wetenhall, the then celebrated stockbroker, who went to live in Kennington Lane next door [to] The Pilgrim [an inn], and who took it in his head to keep there—near London—a pack of fox hounds.[19] His dress was as peculiar as his manners and character. On Change [i.e., at the stock exchange] he always wore a light drab coat, breeches and stockings with a red waistcoat, brass buttons and a clergyman's shovel hat.

He had other peculiarities as those, on Change or in his home. For instance, being very fond of music, and his eldest daughter afterwards Mrs Nairne,[20] my father's best pianoforte scholar, Haydn when in England upon hearing her play dedicated 3 sonatas to her.[21]

---

[19] According to the Guildhall Library, which holds the stock exchange archive, the exchange's printed list of securities and their prices was published twice weekly from about 1803 under Wetenhall's 'control'.

[20] Edward Wetenhall married Elizabeth Booth on 11 February 1776, and their daughter Ann Wetenhall, presumably their eldest daughter, was christened on 17 October 1777 (IGI). Probably she was the 'Miss Wittenhall' who in 1791 subscribed (as did CFH) to Cecilia Maria Barthelemon's *Three Sonatas for the Piano-forte*, see note 138 below. No record of Ann Wetenhall's marriage has been located, and the spelling of her married name is uncertain. CEH appears to have written 'Nairn' on top of a previously written letter 'C', suggesting conjecturally that her husband might have been the Charles Nairne who is listed in *Kent's Original London Directory* (London, 1817) as a stockbroker at Hercules Passage, Threadneedle Street.

[21] CEH's statement appears to be incorrect, as no sonatas by Haydn are known to have been dedicated to a Miss Wetenhall (although, by 'dedicated', CEH conceivably could have meant 'inscribed'). However, a work entitled *Three Sonatas for the Piano Forte or Harpsichord dedicated by permission to Miss Wetenhall*, by Leopold Koželuch, Bohemian composer, 1747–1818, op. 38, was published in London by John Bland and was entered at Stationers' Hall on 9 March 1793. Miss Wetenhall is not mentioned in the correspondence between Koželuch and his English publishers transcribed in Christa Flamm, 'Ein Verlegerbriefwechsel zur Beethovenzeit', in *Beethoven-Studien*, Österreichische Akademie der Wissenschaften Veröffentlichungen der Kommission für Musikforschung, v 11, Vienna, 1970, p 57–110. I am grateful to Dr Christa

But Wetenhall's singular character was such that, in his own house, although appearing a great tyrant and hauteur, [he] always patronised musical men. He would generally go to Vauxhall on the most rainy night of the season—take all his family and invite a few neighbours, pay for them all, and his great satisfaction was that [of] knowing many of the orchestra, who were continually invited to his home. He would sit in the large room opposite the orchestra and encore as many things as he liked, and often done for the pleasure of seeing the arrogance of the very men whom he used to invite to his house, obliged to obey the dictates of the visitors. He who alone was paramount in his orders while they at the same time understood it as a joke, but rather a hard one to take, of a cold evening and blowing night.

He would particularly encore Dignum's songs,[22] who was a very fat and selfish man and wore a three-cornered cocked hat. Mrs Mountain[23] was then, with Mrs Bland,[24] a great favourite at these [Vauxhall] Gardens. Soon after this time Mr Wetenhall lost his son fox hunting near Box Hill, who was so severely injured by a fall in leaping that he died a few months afterwards.[25]

Harten for suggesting that Bland arranged the dedication to Miss Wetenhall without referring to Koželuch, who lived in Vienna from 1778 and never visited England. It is conceivable that Bland, who published several of Haydn's works, and with whom Haydn stayed on his first arrival in London in January 1791, had asked Haydn to suggest a suitable dedicatee, although no evidence of this has been found. Haydn left London for Vienna in July 1792 and did not return until February 1794 (see H. C. Robbins Landon, *Haydn in England, 1791–1795*, London, 1976, p 31, 178, 231). Landon (*Haydn: The Years of 'The Creation', 1796–1800*, London, 1977, p 541) notes that 'Haydn and Koželuch were not on intimate terms', so presumably Koželuch did not ask Haydn to recommend a dedicatee.

[22] Charles Dignum, composer and singer, *c*1765–1827.

[23] Sarah Mountain, soprano, 1768–1841.

[24] Maria Theresa Bland, singer and actress, 1770–1838.

[25] The IGI records only one son of Edward and Betty Wetenhall: Edward Wetenhall [Jr], who was christened on 6 May 1779. I am grateful to Michael Turner of the Bodleian Library for the information that this son was apprenticed at Stationers' Hall on 6 August 1793 to a stationer named Thomas Smith. In the apprenticeship record, Edward Wetenhall [Sr] is identified as a stockbroker of

It was here in Pratt Street that Haydn was invited by my father, with [Domenico] Dragonetti, the prima contrabass at the Opera House,[26] to meet Salomon and the elder Bridgetower[27]—a very dark creole or Indian, for he was dressed in robes—and which struck me with such astonishment or fear when I was brought in after dinner— that it occasioned Haydn, the great and immortal composer of *The Creation*, to take me upon his knee, and this I never forgot. Although I did not know Haydn from any other, excepting he appeared to me a neat good-natured old gentleman with ruffles at his wrists and bosom and a powdered wig with curls on the side, seated next [to] my mother. And, perceiving my alarm at the oriental-looking blackamoor, he held me the closer, and this made the impression on me. When I told the story some time afterwards, I was informed it was Haydn who held me on his knee. This was the honour that afterwards made so lasting an impression on me.

I soon began to practise and would take a violin, find my own way, and then take delight in teaching my brother Frederick who, poor fellow, was subject to fits. However, we contrived to get on so well that, after my father had given us the movement and fingering, we would astonish him or rather tease him, after his hard day's teaching, to hear us play Schwindl's duets for two violins.[28]

He then began to teach us. I could already read pretty well on the pianoforte, and my father would take delight in making me play the bass part of Corelli's trios,[29] he [playing] the first violin and Frederick [the] second. He

---

Kennington Place, Lambeth. *A Trio for two Violins and Violoncello* by William Henry Ware (composer, 1777–1828), which was dedicated to Edward Wetenhall Jr, was entered at Stationers' Hall on 20 March 1799, which suggests that he was alive then.

[26] Domenico Dragonetti, double bassist, 1794–1846. He apparently first arrived in London about October 1794 (see Fiona M. Palmer, *Domenico Dragonetti in England (1794–1846)*, Oxford, 1997, p 98). Haydn left England on 15 August 1795 and never returned (see Landon, *Haydn in England, 1791–1795*, p 319).

[27] Frederick Augustus Bridgetower, father of George Polgreen Bridgetower, violinist, 1778–1860.

[28] Friedrich Schwindl, composer, 1737–1786.

[29] Arcangelo Corelli, Italian composer, 1653–1713.

1794 [to] 1798

already began to show me how to play the common chord[30] where I saw a '3' or nothing marked.[31] Commenced thorough bass. And from these simple trios we would try Handel's oratorios, all three playing out of the same book. He then began to speak of sending for all [of] Mozart's works. I had seen some few things and was all impatient for them to arrive.[32] My father would play bits of sonatas resembling his quartettos, I mean his violin quartettos.[33] I began to think what we should do for a Tenore[34] performer, particularly when he [CFH] spoke of his [Mozart's] pianoforte trio with accompaniment for clarinet and viola.[35] He said I should learn that. Fred[erick] and his friend [Carl] Hartman, a celebrated clarinet player,[36] were to be invited when I have learned to play it.

A Tenore was bought and sent home, but I was determined to try what a Tenore was intended for, in a different clef too, between the bass and violin, and I soon found how it was to be tuned. And so, without a word to my father, [I] could learn or teach myself the notes, as they answered on the book to the positions on the instrument, but I was as long learning the names of the notes on the book (although I could very soon play common easy quartetto passages). I was learning the bass notes as a child under the Mr Page, whom I shall never forget. I surprised my father by instead of practising the pianoforte part of Mozart's trio when they arrived as I had been

---

[30] A triad.

[31] CEH is describing a standard practice of fundamental-bass notation.

[32] CFH's arrangement for harpsichord or pianoforte, violin and violoncello of four movements from Mozart's 'Sinfonia for a grand orchestra', i.e., his serenade K. 320, had been published by Longman and Broderip in 1792.

[33] CEH appears to be saying that CFH played extracts from Mozart's string quartets.

[34] A viola.

[35] K. 498. An edition of this work entitled *Trio for the Piano-forte or Harpsichord with Accompaniments for a Violin or Clarinet & Tenor* was published in London by Longman and Broderip in 1788.

[36] Several of Hartman's clarinet performances are listed in Landon, *Haydn in England, 1791–1795, op. cit.*, p 131, 245, 304 and 551.

practising the Tenore. I told him if he would play the pianoforte I would take the Tenore which, although a small one, I found great difficulty in grasping. He laughed and thought me joking. I made the attempt (and an attempt only it was), for the presence of Mr Hartman the clarinet player frighted me, and I could not get over my fears.

However, my father found I had been at work and said, this is all very well but, if you want to be great, stick to one instrument. So, greatly disappointed, I was put down to the pianoforte part which, by their great indulgence in giving way, I got through. But when they wanted an easy quartetto—and at that time Pleyel's very easy op. 1 was all I could accomplish[37]—and my Tenore playing was not despised on such occasions but found very useful, particularly when my 3^d brother George[38] began to handle a small violoncello which was bought for him. Here was I at the violoncello as I was at the Tenore. Taught myself from the Lessons I saw my father teaching my brother and was soon found out trying experiments—another instrument being brought into the house. I soon discovered among my father's music early violoncello duettos by Crosdill,[39] and got up every morning by six o'clock to practise duettos with my brother, before we went to school.

But the first boys' school I went to was a Mr Goodall, where I became acquainted with Charles Neate, the now celebrated pianoforte performer and instructor.[40] What struck me as so very peculiar was his drinking such immoderate quantities of cold water. This was a day

---

[37] Ignace Joseph Pleyel's six string quartets, op. 1, composed in 1782–1783, were published in London in several editions.

[38] George John Horn was born on 10 October 1790 and was baptised on 8 November 1790 at St Marylebone (copy of baptism record, British Library, Oriental and India Office, L/MIL/9/115/64-65).

[39] John Crosdill, 'cellist, c1751–1825. In 1782 he was appointed chamber musician to the Royal Household, where presumably he met CFH.

[40] Charles Neate, composer and pianist, 1784–1877. CEH consistently spelled his surname 'Neat'. Emily Anderson mentions (in 'Charles Neate: a Beethoven friendship', in Walter Gerstenberg *et al* (eds.), *Festschrift Otto Erich Deutsch zum 80. Geburtstag*, Kassel, 1963, p 196–197) that Neate, when a boy, lived in Lambeth with his first piano teacher, James W. Windsor (1776–1853).

school in Pratt Street and, in the summertime, there was a large can of cold pump water for the boys, and this boy Neate, although very small but my senior by 3 or 4 years, yet he would drink at that age (about 10) a whole quart of this cold water at a draught.[41]

About this time Pinto, an extraordinary talented boy on the violin,[42] came to take lessons in thorough-bass of my father, and we—my brothers, self and Pinto—often played quartets in the garden, to the infinite amusement of the neighbours, who crowded the windows to hear us.[43]

We soon made friends. My father moved into a smaller house on account of the dreadful scarcity coming on in England. The revolution in French[44] and the death of Louis [X]VIth had its effects in England.[45] I can remember, when being taken to Pratt Street as a child, Edward Wetenhall's expression at the dinner table when the news arrived that the king had escaped.[46] He said, 'Well, he shall have the last bottle of wine out of my cellar if he comes to England'. Bread got very dear: if I remember, near two shillings a loaf. The richest families eat potatoes instead.

My father, with 7 children all small,[47] his mother and sister and two or three servants, thought proper to curtail his expenses, and we

---

[41] In fact, Neate was two years older than CEH.

[42] George Frederick Pinto, violinist, pianist and composer, 1785–1806.

[43] In his *Reminiscences* (now British Library Add Ms 27593), written in 1836, Samuel Wesley stated (f 42) that he was introduced to J. S. Bach's '48' by Pinto. No confirmation of this statement has been found, but it is plausible that Pinto could have become acquainted with the '48' during his lessons with CFH.

[44] i.e., in France.

[45] Louis XVI was executed on 21 January 1793.

[46] Louis XVI and his family escaped from Paris on 20 June 1791 but were captured at Varennes-en-Argonne on 22 June.

[47] The sons were CEH, Frederick Thomas, George John and William James (born 30 July 1792 and baptised 25 September 1792 at St James, Piccadilly); the daughters were Henrietta Elizabeth, Louisa Maria (born 15 January 1794 and baptised 23 April 1794 at St Mary's, Lambeth) and Sophia (born 28 January 1797 and baptised 1 January 1798 at St Mary's, Lambeth). I am grateful to Colin Gowing and Audrey Dedman for obtaining copies of the baptism records

moved in[to] China Row, Lambeth. Once here, [in] Charles Street, my brother Frederick and I would amuse ourselves by playing trios of a Sunday afternoon to my grandmother (and aunt).[48] And my grandmother, being a real democratic German, did not hesitate to bring the servants in to hear us youngsters playing trios.

And, upon one of these occasions, I remember we found Beethoven's 3 pianoforte trios dedicated to Salieri.[49] We tried them over, gave our opinion as rather singular but did not much relish them. They produced upon me somewhat the same effect as the music of Giornovichi[50] or Gelinek's 'Variations'.[51] I could not see that peculiar beauty in them which since I have.

Charles Neate was full of fun at that time, and we would often impose upon my poor grandmother, who never knew a note of music, but used sometimes [to] say 'Dere yonfff Spieler ist like de Hund un Kats', and she would look angry when we, the performers, would drown in our jokes and go into a well-known air, *Lieber Augustin*. She would then smile and cry out 'Das its Sheriee' and, taking up one of the children, would begin to dance with them the old German dance of slapping the hands. And, when we left off, she would continue singing, and often [we] spent a pleasant evening with her, whose spirits at times were almost too great, for they would bring on a fit of coughing. None of us had such influence over her as my brother Frederick. She used to watch him, when ill or well. The fits he was subject to I suppose gave him this preference. She used to call him 'Minne lieber Frederick'.

She soon died of a dropsy and for many days could eat nothing. Nothing they brought her pleased her. When I thought of some

---

of several of CFH's children.

[48] i.e., CFH's mother, Sophia Dorothea Horn, and one of CFH's sisters (probably Mary Horn, the music teacher mentioned later in this memoir).

[49] CEH presumably is referring to Beethoven's 1794–1795 piano trios, op. 1, which were not dedicated to Salieri, and perhaps was confused by the circumstance that Beethoven's 1797–1798 violin sonatas, op. 12, were dedicated to him.

[50] Giovanni Mane Giornovichi, Italian violinist and composer, *d*1804.

[51] Josef Gelinek, Czech composer, 1758–1825.

raspberry tarts I went to her bedside and begged her to try one. She did, and burst out crying, exclaimed 'Minne Carl—du hast made me well'. However, she died a few days after,[52] and we were sent, without knowing the cause, to my grandfather [John] Dupont [at] Chelsea. And a servant coming one day with some new clothes for me to be taken to the Ancient Concerts[53]—my father always having a ticket sent by command from the Lord Chamberlain and, on this occasion, one for me.[54] When the bundle was opened the black suit set poor Frederick and myself off into a flood of tears and, added to which, I was only sent for, and to leave him who was so fond of her just gone, was another trial. However, he was comforted by being told he was to go home the next day. I was dressed for the first time in black and went off with the servant to some house near the Haymarket where I met my father in deep mourning. This again was something melancholy and new, for we had never known the loss of a friend or was too young to know what such a loss was.

However, I was taken into the Concert Rooms and remember my father bowing to the Royal Box, and the princesses were always affable and recognised their master. I was told to look up and do the same, and remember two of the princesses talking to each other, laughing and nodding, but as I had never seen them, to my recollection, particularly in such a conspicuous situation, I thought no more of them than anybody else and, when they nodded, why I nodded too. But the King and Queen came in. Then I found everything was hushed and, when they sat down, the orchestra start[ed] up the overture to *The Messiah*, the first orchestral and choral performance I had ever heard, if I remember correctly. Mr Harrison[55] sang the opening 'Comfort ye my people', and I thought

---

[52] Sophia Horn 'of China Row', CFH's mother, was buried on 30 March 1798 at St Mary's, Lambeth. I am grateful to Colin Gowing for this information.

[53] The Concerts of Antient Music, held at this time in the Tottenham Street Rooms.

[54] James Cecil (1748–1823), 7th Earl of Salisbury, created 1st Marquess of Salisbury in 1789, was Lord Chamberlain of the [royal] Household from 1783 to 1804.

[55] Samuel Harrison, tenor, 1760?–1812.

him a very quiet singer and wonder[ed] why such a person was allowed in such a great assembly to stand up and sing with such unmeaning character, for I had remembered trying Handel's oratorios, and thought there were certain passages that no human voice could give sufficient power and expression to. Indeed, many parts of *The Messiah* set me to sleep, excepting such a chorus as 'If [blank]'.[56] I immediately inquired if they were not all angry with each other.

And, as regards Mr Harrison, I never could appreciate his singing or his style till I some years afterwards stood near him while he was rehearsing one of Handel's quiet songs. I then found out his great excellence as a chaste vocalist and, although too quiet and intimate for a concert room, particularly with an orchestra, yet with a pianoforte or in a private room his small delivery was the most perfect thing that I ever heard which, of course, some years afterwards I had many opportunities of witnessing.

However, *The Messiah* coming to the close, the Hallelujah Chorus at the end of the second part during which the King, Queen and Royal Family always stood up with the whole room, and the spirited Chorus of the 3rd part, kept me sufficiently awake to make me remember, to this day, its performance and the effect of the singers and chorus had upon me. My age was such that I took little interest in the singers and only liked and remembered it as the first grand musical performance I had ever heard, and I was only then about 10 years old.

I was then sent back to school, which had been changed from the Pratt Street day school to South Lambeth as a weekly boarder, and where the only boys I became attached to was George and John Gibson—the latter afterwards became my eldest sister's husband[57]— and Henry and John Laing.[58] The first [is] now Dr [Henry] Laing of

---

[56] 'If God be for us'. CEH left space in his manuscript to complete the title but did not return to do this.

[57] John Thomas Gibson, officer of the Indian army, 1785–1851, married CEH's sister Henrietta in 1811; they had nine children (British Library, Oriental and India Office, Service Record—Madras, L/MIL/11/38 p 331 personal ID 18).

[58] CEH consistently wrote 'Lang' for 'Laing'.

Brighton,[59] and John [is] a merchant of London.[60] Dr Laing became the instructor and master of my sister's children upon her first visit to England after being with her husband 10 years in India, and her second son, Dockley Gibson, being educated for a clergyman, married the daughter of John Laing.[61] Thus we all schoolfellows became afterward related by the marriages of my sister's and the Laings' children.

My schooldays were nothing for me to boast of, for the master of the academy being fond of music, and my father desiring that my brother and self should have the use of a pianoforte and our violins whenever we had nothing to do, consequently we were favoured in our studies, and brought out on all occasions of our master Mr Wright's private evening parties to amuse them and neglect our studies from having let up late the evening before. However, the Gibsons and the Laings were our constant visitors as boys from school on Sundays, and this was continued till their departure from school for good and to become cadets for the Indian Service.[62]

I now took to practising hard and remember Charles Neate—who played Dussek's[63] concertos at the Oratorios then taking place at

---

[59] Henry Laing, clergyman and boarding-school master, *bap*1784–*c*1872. He was admitted to Trinity Hall, Cambridge, in 1802, received the degree LL.D. from Cambridge in 1816, and lived at Brighton from 1842 to 1870. See John Archibald Venn, *Alumni Cantabrigienses*, part 2, Cambridge, 1954.

[60] David Laing, the father of Henry and John Laing (*bap*1785) and their brother Thomas Laing (*bap*1773), had a cork manufacturing business at 1 Great Tower Street, London in 1794 (Venn, *op. cit.*; *Kent's Directory for the Year 1794*, London, 1794). The business passed to Thomas and John Laing, who are listed at the same address in the *Post Office Annual Directory* (London, 1814) and at another address in the *Post Office London Directory* (London, 1834).

[61] Charles Dockley Gibson, chaplain, 1818–1869, graduated B.A. from St John's College, Cambridge, in 1841, and married Louisa Laing (1816–1903) in 1842. See Venn, *op. cit.*, and Sidney James McNally, *The Chaplains of the East India Company*, London, 1976, a typescript (of which a photocopy is in the British Library) of India Office Records.

[62] John Thomas Gibson became an officer cadet in the Indian Army in 1800 (British Library, Oriental and India Office, Cadet Papers, L/MIL/9/111 f 625).

[63] Jan Ladislav Dussek, composer, pianist and music publisher, 1760–1812.

October 31st 1823.

Charles Frederick Horn a native of
Germany, came to London in the year
1782 where he was kindly received by his
late Excellency the Saxon Ambassador
Count Brühl, and recommended by him
to the late Marquis of Stafford to assist
to instruct in Music the Young Ladys
the [...] Lady Leveson Gower & & then
dedicated his first work Six Sonatas for
the Piano Forte to Lady Charlotte [...] Her Grace
the present Duchess of Beaufort

In the Year 1789 he had the distinguished
honor of being recommended by Lady Car-
teret & Mr Clementi [...]
line [...] to Her late Majesty the Queen Charlotte
to instruct [...] the Princesses in Music when he did
until the Year 1811, [...] the [...]
was also commanded to attend twice a
week on her Majesty from [...] 1789 to
October 9th 1793 — [...]

Mr Horn has written [...] Instrument
Sonatas & & Themes [...] Variation with an
Accompaniment for Flute or Violin & & &c

Extract of Charles Frederick Horn's 31 October 1823 letter to the compiler of the *Biographical Dictionary of Musicians* (by permission of the Department of *Special Collections, Glasgow University Library*)

MR HORN,

AS BEAUCHAMP.

Engraved by T. WOOLNOTH. from a drawing by WAGEMAN.

Pub.d 1823.by Simpkin & Marshall. Stationers Ct & Chapple Pall Mall.

Charles Edward Horn as Beauchamp in *Rich and Poor (by permission of the Harry Ransom Humanities Research Center, University of Texas at Austin)*

CHARLES E. HORN, AS CASPER, IN " DER FREISCHÜTZ."

Charles Edward Horn as Caspar in *Der Freischütz (by permission of the Harry Ransom Humanities Research Center, University of Texas at Austin)*

Playbill of benefit for Matilda Ray in which Charles Edward Horn performed, Theatre Royal, Cheltenham, 30 June 1810 *(by courtesy of the Cheltenham Art Gallery and Museum)*

Covent Garden Theatre in Lent[64] under the Ashley[s][65]—was practising very hard indeed, so much so that when ever I called on him he was hard at it, while I had treated it as an amateur. But, remembering that it was likely to be my profession, I became jealous of Neate and set to work myself. My father was too much engaged to know what was doing at home, but in the midsummer holidays, after these exhibitions of Neate at the Oratorios where I went with him to hear him play, I set to work and practised many days 10 hours, only stopping to eat my meals. This self-application of mine got to my father's ears and he watched, instructed and encouraged me till we removed again, to Queens Buildings, Brompton.

My sisters were put to a school in Sloane Street, Miss Babbington,[66] and I, becoming now 15 or 16 years old, was employed to assist my father in instructing some of the younger ladies in their notes and commencement. I was encouraged on this occasion by having a blind pupil judge me, who set every piece down by brass pegs to correspond with crotchets and quavers, for which I had one guinea a quarter, once a week. Well, this was a beginning, and I always bought with this guinea some books, pens and paper. However, before the first year was over I had another pupil offered me in the City, two Miss Cohens in Goodmans Fields,[67] for 5 shillings a lesson, two taking a lesson in one hour, twice a week. This was a fortune. I no sooner received my appointment than I proposed buying everything myself that I wanted for wearing apparel.

---

[64] CEH apparently is referring to Neate's first public performances, which were of pianoforte concertos at the Covent Garden Oratorio concerts on 28 February and 4 April 1800.

[65] John Ashley, bassoonist and oratorio manager, 1734–1805, and his sons.

[66] Probably the 'Mrs Babbington' of Sloane Street who subscribed to Domenico Corri's *The Singers Preceptor, or Corri's Treatise on Vocal Music*, London, 1810. 'Miss Babington' is listed at 103 Sloane Street in *Boyle's Court and Country Guide ... corrected up to 18 January 1805* (London, 1805) and also in *Boyle's Court and Country Guide ... for January, 1812* (London, 1812).

[67] The Misses Cohen perhaps were daughters of Hymen Cohen, a merchant of Mansell Street, Goodmans Fields.

One thing I remember relating. My friends the Cohens—who were always very kind to me from the recommendations of the Goldsmids, where my father was instructor[68]—a friend of Cohen's, a professional man, a German Jew who played well on the violin and was requested to choose a pianoforte for my pupils and, what makes it worse, the pianoforte to be chosen I was to go and introduce this violin player. I did so. When the instrument was chosen at Broadwood's old Mr B.[69] was present, and the price was fixed at 35 guineas, the commission to be given to Mr Cohen's kind friend. But imagine my surprise when we were going away, that the violin friend of Mr Cohen's stopped me at the door and asked me if Mr Broadwood would have any objection to charge Mr Cohen 40 guineas for the piano, that he might have 5 guineas more than was his due as commission, from his friend and patron—upon which I told him to speak himself. I heard Mr Broadwood say, 'I don't care what you charge your friend, so long as you bring me the price I ask you as a professional man', and all I knew of the matter was that Mr Cohen asked me some days after if I did not think it was a splendid instrument for 40 guineas, turning round to his children saying 'now, my dears, with such a master and such an instrument you must be the greatest performers in the world'. 'Such a master' was the salvo that stopped my replying, as I was greatly inclined to expose this transaction, and only replied, 'his friend no doubt knew its value or would not have recommended it'.

---

[68] Presumably the family of Abraham Goldsmid, financier, 1756?–1810, to whom, on 24 December 1805, CFH dedicated his composition *Trafalgar, An Heroic Song; as sung by Mr C. E. Horn, Junr at the Harmonic Society* (copy in Bodleian Library, Oxford, Mus. 5.c.77(5)). In his dedication, CFH said that he had been honoured with Goldsmid's friendship 'for a series of years'. The Cohen and Goldsmid families were acquainted: both supported Jewish charities and other activities. The Harmonic Society, which held musical performances at the London Tavern, had been established by Anton or Anthony Schick, a merchant from Germany who was naturalised in 1799; its secretary was John Sterland (c1769–1854), a musical amateur. See 'Memoirs of the metropolitan concerts', *The Harmonicon*, November 1832, p 246–247, and Alec Hyatt King, 'The quest for Sterland – 2; Sterland, the Harmonic Society and Beethoven's fourth symphony', in his *Musical Pursuits*, London, 1987, p 126–136.

[69] John Broadwood, piano manufacturer, 1732–1812.

My teaching at Mr Cohen's and Miss Babbington's went on, and my visits in Goodmans Fields were often [di]versified by visiting old Mr Gibson[70] and his daughters for, although my schoolfellows and associates were in India, it was delightful to go a[nd] see the old place we used to see our friends in.

I was now introduced to Mrs Macdonald, the wife of the Army Agent's[71] and friends to Mr E[dward] Stephenson, my godfather. I had her kin as pupils, one with a very fine voice who became afterwards a pupil of the celebrated Naldi,[72] and came out as a professional singer under the patronage of Sir V. Gibbs and his Lady, Sir Vicary being then Solicitor General.[73] I was introduced by Mrs Macdonald to Sir [blank] Macdonald and their family at the house.[74] I was much surprised to find, although he was a very excellent performer and had a magnificent instrument,[75] yet when we, after

---

[70] Bowes John Gibson, *bap*1744, father of John Thomas Gibson and George Gibson.

[71] Macdonald, Army Agent, Pall Mall Court, is listed without a first name in the *Royal Kalendar* (London, 1799) and the *Royal Kalendar* (London, 1809). *Boyle's Court and Country Guide ... for January, 1812* (London, 1812) lists Angus Macdonald, Army Agent, at 4 Pall Mall Court.

[72] Giuseppe Naldi, Italian bass singer, 1770–1820.

[73] Sir Vicary Gibbs, judge, 1751–1820, was knighted in 1805 and was solicitor general in 1805–1806. He married Frances Cerjat Mackenzie (*d*1843) in 1784.

[74] From the remainder of this paragraph it is clear that CEH's reference is to Godfrey Macdonald, naval officer and lieutenant general, 1775–1832, from 1814 Godfrey Bosville, from 1824 Godfrey Bosville Macdonald 3rd Baron Macdonald of Sleat. Lord Macdonald and his wife had 11 children.

[75] Later, in 1810, Lord Macdonald purchased the Stradivari 'Mara' violoncello for 200 guineas, and he subsequently bought, and his name was given to, the Stradivari 'Macdonald' violin (see W. Henry Hill *et al*, *Antonio Stradivari: his Life and Work (1644–1737)*, London, 1902, especially p 266–267, where Macdonald is incorrectly referred to as 'General Boswell'). Like Macdonald, Edward Stephenson collected stringed instruments and owned what was described as 'perhaps the best and the most valuable collection of Cremona violins of any private gentleman in England' (W. T. Parke, *Musical Memoirs*, London, 1830, v 1 p 301), including three violins and one viola made by Stradivari (Herbert K. Goodkind, *Violin Iconography of Antonio Stradivari 1644–1737*, Larchmont, New York, 1972, p 761).

dinner, went to play a duetto, neither of his bows could be found till after a long search—in the kitchen drawers, among the knives and forks, his bows were found. His excuse was that the children were home from school. When I found in years afterwards this was the same Lord Macdonald in whose great coat, found after the fight at Waterloo, a quartetto of Mozart's discovered the owner of the coat. His love for music was such that he had a servant in all his marches to take care of the music and instruments, that he might practise in camp.[76]

What with visiting musical families, singing a little, and being an expert performer on piano, violin and

1805

violoncello, I contrived to make a very excellent connection. Among them were Col. Wilson of Chelsea College,[77] Miss Grahams—Lord Abercorn's nieces,[78] Mrs Richardsons,[79] [and] Mr Roberts of Belgrave Place.[80] The introduction at Chelsea College procured me the deputyship organist to the celebrated Dr [Charles] Burney,[81] where I continued to officiate for some time. With the Miss Grahams I went to a grand *déjeuner à la fourchette*[82] of Sir J[ohn] Soane's, the

---

[76] In *A Romantic Chapter in Family History*, London, 1911, Alice Bosville Macdonald notes (p 21) that Lord Macdonald took his 'beloved violoncello' with him to the Peninsular War.

[77] Presumably Lt Col. John Wilson, deputy treasurer of Chelsea College, *d*1812.

[78] Nieces (presumably 'Misses Graham', not further identified) of John James Hamilton, 9th Earl of Abercorn and 1st Marquess of Abercorn, 1756–1818.

[79] Presumably 'Misses Richardson'.

[80] Not identified.

[81] Charles Burney, Mus. Doc., historian of music, 1726–1814. His 17 October 1808 letter to Samuel Wesley (Yale University, Beinecke Library, Osborn mss 3, Box 5, folder 319, summarised in Michael Kassler and Philip Olleson, *Samuel Wesley (1766–1837): A Source Book*, Aldershot, 2001, p 242–243), confirms that Lt Col. Wilson, Burney's neighbour at Chelsea College (the Royal Hospital, where Burney lived and of which he was organist, although the organist duties were carried out mainly by deputies), introduced him to CEH.

[82] A breakfast that included the service of meat.

architect,[83] near Harrow, where I met the Duke of Sussex[84] and was introduced to many of the nobility. I remember hearing here [John] Braham[85] for the first time in private and, being obliged to sing after this little great man, made me feel what fear was to sing at a large private party for the first time. For we are not quite so sensitive in our young days, and I believe [that this] gives many a person a chance of success which otherwise in private life never would have come out.

The Battle of Trafalgar with Nelson's death was now the topic of the day[86] and, on the Night of Illuminations,[87] I met my uncle John Dupont at 8 in the evening, bringing the melancholy news of the death of my grandfather Dupont. I did not let him go home but kept the secret the whole evening, as everything appeared to be so gay. A violent storm of rain, thunder, lightning put an end to the rejoicing sooner than expected, so I went to bed with the secret, determined not to say anything till the next morning, and then told my father only— that his experience might best know how to break it to my mother. However, he said 'tell your mother', and left the house. This done, I reflected on this second loss, and went to the pianoforte to practise.

About this time Charles Incledon, the celebrated vocalist living in Brompton Crescent,[88] called one day on my father and asked him if he would allow me to accompany him on the pianoforte in his entertainment *The Wandering Melodist*; that he would pay my expenses and give me 3 guineas—which I thought a great deal too much, when it would cost me nothing to go and see the country parts, for I had never travelled. This circumstance induced me to think of

---

[83] Sir John Soane, R.A., 1753–1837.

[84] Augustus Frederick, 1773–1843, sixth son of George III.

[85] John Braham, tenor, 1777–1856.

[86] Admiral Horatio Nelson, 1758–1805, was killed in the Battle of Trafalgar on 21 October 1805.

[87] Perhaps about the time of Nelson's funeral in London on 9 January 1806.

[88] Charles Incledon, tenor, 1763–1826. *Boyle's Court and Country Guide ... for January, 1812* (London, 1812) gives his address as 13 Brompton Crescent.

theatre. In these peregrinations I first saw, at Cheltenham,[89] M– R–,[90] a beautiful young actress playing at her father's theatre,[91] when all the boy's and girl's flirtation took place,[92] which cause ended so unfortunately in years after.[93]

---

[89] Incledon's 'new entertainment', which CEH accompanied on 11 September 1806 in the Lower Assembly Rooms, Cheltenham, was called *Hospitality, or The Harvest Home* rather than *The Wandering Melodist*. (A copy of the playbill is in the Cheltenham Art Gallery and Museum.)

[90] i.e., Matilda Ray, whom CEH married in 1810 (see below). For her career see 'Memoir of Mrs Horn', *The Theatrical Inquisitor and Monthly Mirror for May 1816* (London, 1816) p 322–326, and 'Memoir of Mrs C. Horn', *Oxberry's Dramatic Biography and Histrionic Anecdotes* (London, 1825–1827), v 7 p 17–24. Both of these memoirs incorrectly state that she married CEH in 1811. According to the first memoir, she was born at Pool[e], Dorsetshire, on 21 January 1792. However, in her 18 August 1810 marriage licence allegation (now in the Lambeth Palace Library), she was said to be 'upwards of 19 years but under the age of 21 years'. I thank Peter Ray for the latter information.

[91] The actors Edward Ray and George Collins Gibson were lessees of theatres in Cheltenham and elsewhere. See Anthony Denning, *Theatre in the Cotswolds: the Boles Watson Family and the Circencester Theatre*, London, 1993, p 76.

[92] In his 17 October 1808 letter (*op. cit.*), Charles Burney told Samuel Wesley that CEH had been 'advised to go to Cheltenham' [spa] because his health was delicate. Burney added that CFH sometimes substituted for CEH as deputy organist of Chelsea College when CEH was unavailable.

[93] CEH's marriage with Matilda was difficult. They appear to have been separated in 1817 when he took up the Dublin engagement described later in this memoir, but were reconciled by 28 October 1822, when CEH told James Winston (*earlier* James Bown, actor and theatre manager, 1774–1843) that Matilda's brother had convinced him 'that all reports of her conduct were false'. However, on 12 November 1826, CEH again had 'settled to be separated from his wife' (see Alfred L. Nelson and Gilbert B. Cross (eds.), *Drury Lane Journal: Selections from James Winston's Diaries*, London, 1974, p 57, 136). On 17 March 1838, CEH married Mary Anne Horton, mezzo-soprano and singing teacher at St James's Episcopal Church, Richmond, Virginia, USA (*The Sun*, Baltimore, 23 March 1838, p 3; the church register is now Accession 21645 in the Library of Virginia, Richmond). Mary Anne Horton was born at Birmingham in 1811, the same year as CEH's son Charles. A brief, somewhat inaccurate account of her career is given in Frederic Boase, *Modern English Biography*, Truro, 1892, v 1 col. 1537. She subsequently married a Mr Züst (before 2 August 1874, as a letter by her of that date in the Harvard Theatre Collection is signed 'M. A. Züst'), and died at Morrisania, then in Westchester

And I became fond of going to hear operas at Drury Lane. Saw an opera called *Kais*[94] in which Braham and [Nancy] Storace[95] appeared and a Miss Lion.[96] I began to introduce myself among professional men and, playing the violoncello and double bass, by stealth I got engaged at Covent Garden as second contrabass, but found it too confined, with rehearsals and, every night, work. J. Kemble[97] at this time was playing [Shakespeare's] *Henry VII[I]th* when I remember, playing a few bars on the organ in the orchestra in the scene, he was discovered asleep. This also I thought a great compliment to be allowed to do when I was not certain of the instrument or what kind of music was to be played, so I contemplated something soothing and got great credit from the performers in the orchestra, as well as from the great Kemble, the star of London at that time, when I saw *Pizarro*[98] played with the following cast: Rolla – J. Kemble; Alonzo – C. Kemble;[99] Pizarro – George Cooke;[100] Orozembo – Dowton;[101] Elvira – Mrs Siddons;[102] and Cora – Mrs Jordan.[103]

County, New York, on 6 January 1887. (I thank Peter Ray for providing a copy of her death notice in *The New York Times*, 7 January 1887, p 5, in which she is called 'Mrs Charles E. Horn Züst'.) Her sister, Priscilla Horton (1818–1895, who married the composer and entertainer Thomas German-Reed, 1817–1888), was prominent on the London stage, both as a contralto and as an actress.

[94] *Kais, or Love in the Deserts* was first performed at Drury Lane on 11 February 1808. The music was by John Braham and William Reeve, composer and actor, 1757–1815.

[95] Anna Selina (called 'Nancy') Storace, soprano, 1765–1817, who lived with John Braham. She was a sister of the composer Stephen Storace, 1762–1796.

[96] Perhaps Elizabeth Sarah Lyon, see note 157 on page 37 below.

[97] John Philip Kemble, actor and theatre manager, 1757–1823.

[98] A play by Richard Brinsley Sheridan, playwright and politician, 1751–1816.

[99] Charles Kemble, actor, 1775–1854, brother of John Philip Kemble.

[100] George Frederick Cooke, actor, 1756–1812.

[101] William Dowton, actor and theatre manager, 1764–1851.

[102] Sarah Kemble Siddons, actress, 1755–1831, sister of John Philip and Charles Kemble.

[103] Dora Jordan, actress, 1761–1861.

It of course was a time when the drama was in its zenith: comedy with Lewis,[104] Emery,[105] Fawcett,[106] J. Johnstone,[107] Mrs Davenport;[108] opera with Braham, [Nancy] Storace, Incledon, Mrs Mountain, Mrs Bland. In the theatre Covent Garden was a treat to go to, Drury Lane no less so with the Rosciuses[109] Mrs Billington,[110] [Michael] Kelly, &c. &c.

At this time I had the pleasure of meeting Mrs Garrick, wife to the far-famed Roscius of the English stage.[111] My father and self were invited to Brook Watson Esq[r] on the Adelphi[112] to dinner. At table, next [to] my father, sat Mrs Garrick, a very old lady.[113] And I remember Mr Watson relating a story how he had contrived to make the prisoners who went to their felon-pew at church more attentive— and a peculiar one for those prisoners who had been forced guests— by placing a coffin and black pall over it. It had the desired effect, for they had been very unruly, although their lives were at stake also.

He telling us, when he was Lord Mayor of London,[114] how he contrived an effect by having a sword cut so that, at a funeral of a peace officer whom he knew, when and where the words uttered 'ashes to ashes and dust to dust' were spoken, he shattered the sword

---

[104] William Thomas Lewis, actor and theatre manager, *d*1811.

[105] John Emery, actor and singer, 1777–1822.

[106] John Fawcett Jr, actor and singer, 1768–1837.

[107] John Henry Johnstone, actor and singer, 1749–1828.

[108] Mary Ann Davenport, actor and singer, 1759–1843.

[109] i.e., the first-rate actors.

[110] Elizabeth Billington, singer and actor, *d*1818.

[111] Eva Maria Garrick, dancer, 1724–1822, widow of David Garrick, actor and theatre manager, 1717–1779.

[112] Sir Brook Watson, merchant, 1735–1807. His address is given as 4 Adelphi Terrace in *Holden's Triennial Directory for 1805–1807* (London, 1805).

[113] Apparently Mrs Garrick was a neighbour of Sir Brook Watson, as her address is given as 5 Adelphi Terrace in *Boyle's Court and Country Guide ... for January, 1812* (London, 1812).

[114] Brook Watson was Lord Mayor of London in 1796 and 1797.

into pieces and which fell into the grave; when (he said) a friend of his told him, 'Garrick could not have acted it better', which pleased the old lady so much that the tears fell from her eyes, and the subject was changed. She soon withdrew with Mrs [Helen] Watson and the gentlemen followed to join them, where we had music and cards, which finished this delightful evening. Mr Brook Watson was an excellent speaker, had been to the West Indies and Charleston in America, where he lost his leg by a shark while bathing when a boy. There was a picture painted[115] and engraved[116] on the subject.

I once remember a piece being performed at Drury Lane of Theodore Hook's,[117] about the time Sir Francis Burdett[118] was taken to the Tower [of London] by an order from the Speaker of the House of Commons,[119] and great excitement with the public was the consequence. I heard already Hook's melodrama was being condemned, the people hissing. While in a cave scene, one of the characters, a Druid, had to call out, 'What says the oracle now?', when Hook, in despair and rage, caught up the speaking trumpet from the man behind the scenes who was to reply. And he [Hook] himself answered through the trumpet to the Druid's question, 'What says the oracle now?'. 'Burdett forever', he called out as loud as he could, threw the instrument down and ran out of the house that was in a confusion, you can better imagine.

I was taken to all the concerts by my quondam godfather Salomon,[120] and remember playing second violoncello at his benefit

---

[115] Watson's loss of a leg in Havana in 1749 is depicted in the painting *Watson and the Shark* by John Singleton Copley the elder (1737–1815). Three examples of this painting, made by Copley in 1778 and 1782, are now in the National Gallery of Art, Washington, D.C., the Museum of Fine Arts, Boston, and the Detroit Institute of Arts.

[116] The mezzotint *Youth Saved from a Shark*, after Copley's portrait, was engraved in 1779 by Valentine Green (1739–1831). A copy is in the Webster Canadian Collection, New Brunswick Museum, Saint John, Canada.

[117] Theodore Edward Hook, writer, 1788–1841.

[118] Politician, 1770–1844.

[119] In 1810.

[120] 'quondam' apparently because Salomon missed CEH's christening

when I happened to be placed on the side where the Prince Regent came in and stood close by me, noticing every note I played. I thought this a great honour, although I was only one of the 60 who made the effects.[121] However, it induced me to practice hard upon an instrument I took up only as an amusement, and so far improved that, when poor Dahmen, the second violoncello,[122] was taken ill of the Opera House, I fulfilled his situation for that season, during which time two operas of Winter's was performed[123] and Mozart's *Clemenza di Tito* was first performed for Mrs Billington's benefit,[124] at which Linly[125] was taken ill and I had to officiate as the principal [violoncello], under the fostering care of the great Dragonetti, contrabass.[126]

The year before this[127] G. Griffin,[128] Mr Alsager,[129] Musgrove,[130] another and myself copied and brought out *Don Juan* of

---

ceremony. See page 9 above.

[121] At this time George, Prince of Wales, was not yet Prince Regent.

[122] Probably Johan Arnold Dahmen, *bc*1760.

[123] Peter von Winter, German composer, *c*1754–1825.

[124] At the King's Theatre, Haymarket, on 27 March 1806. See William C. Smith, *The Italian Opera and Contemporary Ballet in London, 1789–1820*, London, 1955, p 80.

[125] Robert Lindley, 'cellist, 1776–1855, from 1794 to 1851 first violoncello of the King's Theatre.

[126] Lindley and Dragonetti played 'from the same desk at the King's Theatre' (Palmer, *Domenico Dragonetti, op. cit.*, p 101).

[127] Hence in 1805.

[128] George Eugene Griffin Jr, organist and composer, 1781–1863.

[129] Thomas Massa Alsager, 1779–1846, a musical amateur who later became a proprietor of *The Times*. Purday, 'Memoir of C. E. Horn', *op. cit.*, p 558, recounting this event, remarked that 'the late lamented T. Alsager, Esq.' was 'a great patron of music and musicians'.

[130] Rachel Cowgill suggests ('"Wise men from the East": Mozart's operas and their advocates in early nineteenth-century London', in Christina Bashford and Leanne Langley (eds.), *Music and British Culture, 1785–1914*, Oxford, 2000, p 55), that 'Musgrove' may have been W. P. Musgrave, an auctioneer and a musical amateur.

Mozart at Hayward's floor-cloth manufactory,[131] which went off with such éclat that we afterwards ventured upon performing it at the London Tavern,[132] with the following cast: Don Juan – myself; Ottavio – Siboni;[133] Commendatore – Bellamy;[134] Leporello – Naldi; Ann[a] – Miss Feron;[135] Elvira – Miss Hughes;[136] and Zerlina – Miss Griglietti, afterwards Mrs Lazenby, pickle manufacturer!![137]

These events brought me in constant meeting of the principal musical men of the day, and appeared of the greatest use at the musical parties of my aunt, Miss [Mary] Horn, who had at that time a

---

[131] Thomas Hayward, a musical amateur, lent his manufactory for private performances of several Mozart operas. See 'Autobiography of an amateur singer', *The Harmonicon* no. 42 (June 1831) p 135–137, and Alec Hyatt King, 'The quest for Sterland – 3; *Don Giovanni* in London before 1817', in his *Musical Pursuits*, *op. cit.*, p 137–150. The 1805 production described by CEH appears to have been the first performance of *Don Giovanni* in England.

[132] The London Tavern performance, which was the first public performance of *Don Giovanni* in England, took place on 17 April 1809, and was followed on 23 May 1809 by a performance involving many of the same musicians of 'the most beautiful compositions' from *Don Giovanni* at the Hanover Square New Rooms. The cast listed by King (*op. cit.*, p 142) for the 17 April performance, which he derived from newspaper advertisements and 'reasonable assumptions', differs from CEH's memoir in a few respects. Purday, 'Memoir of C. E. Horn', *op. cit.*, p 558, gives another different cast list. As mentioned in footnote 68 above, CEH had earlier sung CFH's song *Trafalgar* at the London Tavern.

[133] Giuseppe Siboni, Italian tenor, 1780–1839.

[134] Thomas Ludford Bellamy, bass singer, 1771–1843.

[135] Elisabeth Feron, singer; on 13 October 1812 she married Joseph Glossop, theatre manager.

[136] Maria Hughes, singer, *b*1789, from 1819 Madame Gatti; see Smith, *The Italian Opera, op. cit.*, p 164.

[137] Elizabeth Augusta Griglietti, soprano; she married the pickle manufacturer George Lazenby in Dublin on 7 September 1817. See T. J. Walsh, *Opera in Dublin, 1798–1820: Frederick Jones and the Crow Street Theatre*, Oxford, 1993, p 167–168.

very considerable share of teaching[138]—B. Sharp,[139] C. Bertram[140] and many young friends making up the musical department for the evenings. The music of Mozart, Haydn, and the operas of Winter, Pucitta[141] and those brought out at this time, were the principal attractions of the evening.

Days, weeks, months and years passed by at that time, when young men or grown boys have little to think of but pleasure. The cares of the world had nothing to do with the passing events of study, beginning to give lessons, forming new acquaintances and all the variety this time of life brings with it, much of which I have forgotten, much remembered, that give[s] pleasure as well as pain in after years, particularly when we feel how much we have neglected at that time of life that would have been of great consolation could I assure myself that I had not neglected [those things]. But so it [is] with the greater part of the world. We know not when we are well off or happy till too late, although there are many circumstances of my life to this time that I could joyfully pass over again.

Musical parties at Mr Attwood's in Pimlico,[142] at Col.

---

[138] Her first name has been determined because 'Miss Mary Horn'—but no Jane Horn (CFH's other sister)—subscribed, as did CFH, to *Three Sonatas for the Piano-forte* by Cecilia Maria Barthelemon *later* Henslowe, a publication entered at Stationers' Hall on 4 February 1791. Mary Horn probably was the 'Miss Horn' who had subscribed in 1786 to CFH's *Six Sonatas*, op. 1, and who had subscribed about 1799 (as did CFH) to the first edition of Haydn's *The Creation*. Perhaps she also was the 'Miss Horn' of Newman Street who subscribed in 1810 to Domenico Corri's *The Singers Preceptor ...*, *op. cit.*

[139] Perhaps Benjamin Sharp, a performer on several musical instruments, 1784–1875, who was a member of the Royal Society of Musicians.

[140] Perhaps a son of the Charles Bertram who had helped CFH when he first arrived in England. See footnote 12 on page 3 above.

[141] Vincenzo Pucitta, Italian composer, 1778–1861, from 1809 to 1814 composer and music director of the King's Theatre.

[142] Thomas Attwood, composer, 1765–1838. He lived at 11 Lower Eaton Street, Pimlico (*Boyle's Court and Country Guide ... for January, 1812*).

Wilson,[143] Col. Graham with Lord Abercorn's family,[144] and many private friends. That part of my life a new and happy world, patronised by all the great and beloved by all. At home I knew no unhappy hours, excepting when I had nothing to employ me. At this time I became acquainted with Col. [John] Macleod of Colbecks who took me to Cheltenham with his family,[145] and where visited His Royal Highness the Duke of Gloucester[146] [and] Lady Moira.[147] Mrs Macleod [was an] aunt [of] the Countess of Loudoun,[148] a very delightful musician and singer[149] to whom I dedicated one of my first

---

[143] See note 77 on page 26 above.

[144] Col. Graham presumably was related to the Misses Graham mentioned in note 78 above.

[145] Col. Macleod (*d*1823), who married his cousin Jane (or Jean) Macleod in 1782, lived from 1807 at Charlton Kings, Gloucestershire, close to Cheltenham. 'Colbecks' was the name of his father's plantation in Jamaica, West Indies. See Edith Humphris and E. C. Willoughby, *At Cheltenham Spa; or, Georgians in a Georgian Town*, London, 1928, p 126–127, and Mary Paget, 'At Cheltenham Spa', *Charlton Kings Local History Society Bulletin* no. 45 (spring 2001) p 32–33. Mrs Macleod was the patron of benefit performances for Matilda Ray at the Theatre Royal, Cheltenham on 30 June 1810 (the bill for which is reproduced facing page 23), and again (when Matilda Ray had become Matilda Horn) on 26 September 1812 and 12 August 1813. Col. Macleod also patronised the latter event. I am grateful to Roger Beacham of the Local Studies Library, Cheltenham, for help in identifying this branch of the Macleod family.

[146] George III's nephew William Frederick, second Duke of Gloucester of the Georgian creation, 1776–1854. According to Humphris and Willoughby, *op. cit.*, p 118, he was a 'constant visitor' to Cheltenham Spa.

[147] Flora Mure-Campbell, 1780–1840. She became Countess of Loudoun in 1786 upon the death of her father James Mure-Campbell (1726–1786, from 1782 5th Earl of Loudoun) and became Lady Moira in 1804 by marrying Francis Rawdon-Hastings, 2nd Earl of Moira (1754–1826).

[148] Jane (or Jean) Macleod was a sister of the countess's mother Flora Macleod (*c*1764–1780), who had married James Mure-Campbell in 1777 and died shortly after the birth of their daughter. (For details of this branch of the Macleod family see Alick Morrison, *The Macleods—The Genealogy of a Clan: Section Four: The Macleods of Lewis with several Septs including the Macleods of Raasay*, Edinburgh, *c*1974, p 15–16, 33–68.) CEH's text is unclear here; he appears to have written 'Laudoff' instead of 'Loudoun'.

[149] The countess's musical studies presumably began before *c*1794, when the

compositions 'The Daughter of Love', and which I think is one of my best songs at this time.[150]

Also I published 6 Canzonets, the words by Lady Blizzard [sic], the celebrated surgeon's first wife.[151] These were dedicated to Her Royal Highness The Princess Amelia, a scholar of my father's, and I remember my only reason given for selecting Her Royal Highness from the 5 princess[es] my father instructed[152] was because she was the youngest and prettiest of the family. I may say this now, as all are gone by, the Duchess of Gloucester[153] and Princess Sophia[154] being the only daughters of George III alive.

A change now took place in my father's movement. He determined on removing from Brompton to Queen Square Bloomsbury N° 25. I had begun to assist him in his teaching. He had recommended me to scholars, and I found that even the few lessons I had received from the celebrated [Venanzio] Rauzzini of Bath,[155] an

---

musical theorist Augustus Frederic Christopher Kollmann (1756–1829)—who, like CFH, was born in Germany and was a pioneer in the introduction of J. S. Bach's music in England—'composed and dedicated' to her his 'Six sonatinas for the piano forte', op. 4.

[150] To this passage CEH added the note printed on p 71 below. 'The Daughter of Love' was published *c*1823 by Willis & Co. in Dublin and was reviewed in the *Quarterly Musical Magazine and Review*, v 6 no. 221 (1824) p 146.

[151] Sir William Blizard, surgeon, 1743–1835. Sir William himself had written the words of CFH's 'heroic song' *Trafalgar*, which CEH had sung a few years earlier (see footnote 68 above), and his contact with the Blizards may have arisen from this circumstance. I am grateful to Jonathan Evans, archivist of the Royal London Hospital, for the information that Sir William married his first cousin Jane Blizard, although it is not known whether this was a first or a later marriage. William Cooke does not mention any wife in his *A Brief Memoir of Sir William Blizard, Knt.*, London, [1835]. No copy of CEH's canzonets with words by Lady Blizard has been located.

[152] i.e., all the royal princesses except Princess Sophia.

[153] Princess Mary, who married William Frederick, Duke of Gloucester, on 22 July 1816. CEH must have stayed in contact with the Duke and Duchess of Gloucester, as she was the patron of his 18 May 1843 concert at the Store Street Rooms in London (programme at Mitchell Library, Sydney, ms A12 letter 33).

[154] 1777–1848. All the other five princesses had died before 1841.

[155] Venanzio Rauzzini, composer and singer, *c*1746–1810. In the article on CEH

Italian of considerable reputation, having been the master and adviser of Braham, Billington, [Nancy] Storace and others.

1808

was as nearly as I can remember the year in which we moved into Queen Square—and with his alteration, which had been recommended by my father's friend and one of my godfathers, Edward Stephenson, banker of Lombard Street, came all future trouble and misfortune.[156] My father's money had been drawn from the Bank, the first hundred pounds I had saved had been used to purchase the furniture of this house which, with taxes, stood 185 pounds a year and, what was worse, I did not feel I could get more a lesson—or that our prospects increased.

An English Opera House was about to open, and Henry Bishop—who had not long been married to Miss Lyon, a singer with a fine sonorous voice[157]—was anxious to make up a company and persuaded me to engage as second singer. Thomas Phillips[158] had been engaged as first, from Dublin, and the same Tom Phillips I had met with James McCaskey in my peregrinations with Incledon while in Ireland. The company was selected and consisted of: Mrs Mountain (whose son I went to school with, and now first clerk at the

---

published in *A Dictionary of Musicians* ... (London, printed for Sainsbury and Co., 1824, v 1 p 375–376), which presumably—like CFH's autobiographical account in Appendix 1 below—was based upon a letter (not located) from CEH to the dictionary's proprietors, CEH is said 'at the age of twenty-two', i.e., in 1808–1809, to have 'resolved to take singing lessons of the celebrated Rauzzini, then residing at Bath, and to whom he accordingly went for that purpose; but, unfortunately, owing to Rauzzini's ill health, of which he soon after died, Horn had not more than five or six lessons'. According to CEH's 1828 sketch of his own career printed in Appendix 2 below, CEH had his last lesson with Rauzzini just a few hours before Rauzzini died on 8 April 1810.

[156] Edward Stephenson's London residence was at 29 Queen Square. The circumstance that CFH and Stephenson were neighbours presumably led to Stephenson's involvement with a projected English translation of Johann Nicholas Forkel's 1802 biography of Bach. See my 'The English translations of Forkel's *Life* of Bach', in Kassler (ed.), *The English Bach Awakening, op. cit.*

[157] Henry Rowley Bishop, composer, 1768–1855, had married Elizabeth Sarah Lyon, singer, 1787–1831, on 30 April 1809.

[158] Tenor, 1774–1841.

Admiralty[159]); Bishop; Phillips; Dowton; Mrs Orger;[160] George Smith;[161] Miss Kelly;[162] Doyle, for opera; for ballet, Miss Luppino later Noble;[163] Oscar Byrne and Miss Smith;[164] D'Egville, ballet master;[165]

1809

Mr Arnold, proprietor and manager;[166] M. P. King, composer, a pupil of my father's;[167] and Mr H. Smart,[168] brother to Sir George Smart,[169] leader of the band.

And with this company I made my first essay on the stage as a dramatic singer in the opera of *Up all Night*, a successful comic opera,[170] being encored in two favourite songs. It was pronounced a successful début, the opera also a hit—Mr T[om] Phillips and Mrs Mountain both being favourites with the public. And thus commenced an English Opera House. The king, George III, sanctioned it, and everything was considered to be most favourable to establishing such a theatre in London.

---

[159] William J. Mountain.

[160] Mary Ann Orger, actress, 1788–1849.

[161] George Smith, actor and singer, *b*1777.

[162] Frances Maria Kelly, actor and singer, 1790–1882, niece of Michael Kelly.

[163] Georgina (also called Rosina) Luppino *later* Noble, dancer, 1778–1832.

[164] Oscar Byrn, dancer, *c*1795–1867. On the Drury Lane playbill for 8 May 1817 'Mrs Oscar Byrne' is identified as 'late Miss Smith'.

[165] James Harvey D'Egville, dancer and choreographer, *c*1770–>1835. I am grateful to Keith Cavers for information about D'Egville's dates.

[166] Samuel James Arnold, dramatist and theatre manager, 1774–1852.

[167] Matthew Peter King, 1773?–1823.

[168] Henry Smart, violinist and composer, 1778–1823. He was the leader of the orchestra of the English Opera House at the Lyceum Theatre from 1809, and from 1812 to 1821 led the orchestra at Drury Lane Theatre.

[169] Conductor and organist, 1776–1867.

[170] *Up all Night, or the Smuggler's Cave*, with words by Samuel James Arnold and music by Matthew P. King, opened at the Lyceum Theatre on 26 June 1809.

All this was accomplished with[out] consulting even my father who, although I knew had a dislike to the stage for my profession, I thought my success would overcome his objections and, [as] he said nothing when he saw my name advertised, I imagined silence gives consent. I was earning at this time from 12 to 15 pounds a week by teaching in the season, and such was my propensity for a public life that I neglected all for 8 pounds a week, sending down every evening my manservant with my dressing box &c. &c. The old stagers and servants about the House thought I must be a very clever person and had a very large salary. I kept my horse and really considered myself to be the only person calculated to be Shining Star.

Drury Lane Theatre and Covent Garden had been burnt down the season before and, strange to say, these destruction[s] followed each other within a very few months, Drury Lane on the first night of H[enry] Bishop['s] opera of *The Circassian Bride* and his first essay as an operatic writer.[171] And he then showed an original talent and style for composition which, had he pursued, would have stood even higher than he now does, in 1848. But he laboured as composer and musical director at Covent Garden afterwards, where he had to compose, select and adapt for whatever was put before him, and that, at times, with such rapid succession that he was obliged to select from the French, Italian and German composers without ceremony to have the different operas, farces and melodramas ready. The managers of theatres generally thinking a composer was like a carpenter or scene painter—that he could hire labour to work his own thoughts out, with the help of saws, hammers; or painting brushes and canvas.

However, to return to the opening of the English Opera House. We had rehearsed for one month. I became acquainted with O.P.[172] and P.S.[173] All were kind and attentive to me, as the only novice of the Company, but as the opening night was advertised my courage began to fail me. The part I had assigned to me was that of Meddle, a

---

[171] *The Circassian Bride* opened at Drury Lane on 23 February 1809. The theatre burnt down the next day.

[172] The side of the stage opposite the prompter.

[173] The prompter's side of the stage.

young country gentleman who was always meddling with other persons' business and neglecting his own. The cast of *Up all Night or The Smuggler's Cave* was: The Admiral – Mr Dowton; his daughter – Mrs Mountain; her friend – Miss Lyon, afterwards Mrs Bishop; Harry – Mr T[om] Phillips; Meddle – myself; Mr Doyle – G[eorge] Smith; made up the *dramatis personæ*.

The overture was played. The chorus of smugglers was over. The scene closed to a number and [i.e., in which] the Admiral and Meddle has to enter P.S. in warm discussion about the daughter. Dowton entered with all his irritable temperament. I had to follow but somehow stuck fast behind the scenes against the walls, immoveable. The Admiral looked behind him, filling up the vacancy—all which I knew was not in his part. At last the prompter, Mr [William] Powell,[174] jumped out of his box and, with the help of one or two of the chorus singers, literally pushed me on the stage, so that I come in with a hiss. A thunder of applause for the young new singer, whose reputation was known as the composer of 'He loves and rides away', words by M. Lewis.[175] I was told by Dowton to bow. I did so, and we commenced.

I got courage and the cue for my song. 'He who feels a lover's anguish' was received with a tremendous encore and burst of encouraging applause. I say 'encouraging' for, with the exception of a quiet sweet voice and thanks for a pause that I might hold it on and be heard, I did not know what I was singing about or if I was singing at all. The words of dialogue and song with the music seemed mechanically to come out of my mouth from the number of rehearsals we had, that I did [not] know whether I was at a rehearsal or before a most crowded and crammed house. The scene ended with a rapid duetto between the Admiral and Meddle which, with Mr Dowton's kind encouragement and assistance, we came off with flying colours.

Each favourite was warmly received. Mr Phillips was highly successful, and the opera concluded with shouts [and] waving

---

[174] 1762–1812.

[175] Matthew Gregory Lewis, writer, 1775–1818, called 'Monk Lewis' after his successful 1796 novel *The Monk*.

1809

of handkerchiefs. And thus was safely ushered the first attempt of establishing an English Opera House. And [the] House was the old Lyceum, near the spot where Exeter 'Change stood and the wild beast[s] were shown. There was no Waterloo Bridge, no wide-opening Strand, for the past was the narrowest of that thoroughfare and wonderful start for traffic. The new opera was played nightly and, after the opera was performed, a short ballet with Mr Noble[176] and Miss Luppino, afterwards Mrs Noble.

A month or 6 weeks elapsed passed before even any thing new was thought of. At length an opera by Mr Addison[177] called *The Siege of Smolensko* was in agitation, in which the same persons had parts.[178] And these two operas were the first season of the English Opera season.

Sheridan's *Duenna* was played this season to give the once-celebrated Quick[179] an opportunity of taking leave of the public. And this, in my early career, should have been a lesson to me as well as other[s]. 'How soon a public favourite is forgotten and sacrificed'— Shakespeare's lines. The audience thought little or nothing then of this. Once said of the public that would set this audience in a roar the moment they heard his squeaking harsh voice.

The duties of the theatre caused me to neglect my teaching. The season closed, and a party was formed to pass a day or two in the country. The place chosen was Hougham in Kent.[180] The party: George Robins, the well-known auctioneer;[181] Charles Mathews the

---

[176] Henry Noble, dancer who performed in London between 1790 and 1814.

[177] John Addison, composer and double bassist, 1765?–1844.

[178] *The Russian Imposter, or The Siege of Smolensko* opened at the Lyceum on 22 July 1809.

[179] John Quick, actor and theatre manager, 1748–1851.

[180] CEH appears to have written 'Hockend' rather than 'Hougham'.

[181] George Henry Robins, 1748–1851. Later he was much concerned with the financial affairs of Drury Lane Theatre and served on that theatre's management subcommittee.

elder and wife;[182] Mr Mountain[183] and wife; T[om] Phillips; Jack as he was called or 'Irish' Johnstone;[184] myself and sister; and, though last not least, W. J. Roper of Snow Hill, and [of] whom much will be said in these memoirs.[185] It will be enough to remark that he was a good-looking sort of Tom and Jerry man,[186] a kind of [blank] in that notorious piece, said very little, but planning all the mischief he could for the amusements of the day.

We met on the time appointed and started [in order] to dine at Hougham, where there was a famous hotel kept by a relative of Johnstone. The day passed off in great glee, with repartee, and the rest of those kind of jokes actors and actresses know how to pass with each other. I was a novice to all this but soon learnt to join them.

So, after dinner, when the champagne and claret with which the landlord supplied us in extra quantities on account of his joining us at dinner, hearing our songs and laughing at the irresistible Mathews, when this had taken such effect as to induce us, the gentlemen, to walk and take the air: well, all started down the High Road and rather hilly. We were standing in the shade in conversation, for it was a beautiful moonshiny night. We saw a coach coming down the hill; it [was] about one in the morning. We all simultaneously decided ourselves to act the part of footpads, and called out 'Stop!' close to the horse's head. The coachman was drawing up when we found it was the Dover Mail going into London, and [the] guard already up in his seat with the blunderbuss aimed at my head, for I was near the coach door. They all burst out laughing, or I should having finished

---

[182] Charles Mathews, actor and singer, 1776–1835, and his second wife Anne Jackson Mathews, actress and author, *c*1782–1869. Their son, Charles James Mathews, 1803–1878, became a well-known actor and in 1838 the second husband of Lucia Elizabetta Bartolozzi Vestris, known as 'Madame Vestris', actress, singer and theatre manager, 1797–1856.

[183] John Mountain, Irish violinist, *b*1766, husband of Sarah Mountain.

[184] John Henry Johnstone, see note 107 above. His nickname 'Irish' came from his skill in playing Irish parts.

[185] Further information about Roper does not appear in CEH's memoirs and has not been located.

[186] i.e., a boisterous, drunken reveller.

my early career and gone off, by a joke. We never thought of our folly till afterwards, when they all congratulated me upon my escape and said I should never do to play Capt Macheath if I did not lay my plans better. However, on reflecting, we all made for our hotel, got soda water and departed each to his rest for the night.

The next morning, after breakfast, while the carriage and horses were putting to, we walk[ed] through the town. Mathews, personifying a maniac, went into a butcher's shop to the knife and chopper, and began so many antics that the man and woman flew out of their house in a fright. That drew all the neighbours round, who were determined, him to the asylum. He ran into the private part of the house, entered a bedroom, tore a sheet off a bed, and wandered about. Roper put on a thick coat, old hat, and came down with a large bunch of keys to represent the keeper of the asylum and, by degrees with our joint assistance, took the madman Mathews and brought him safely to the hotel where a dense crowd of villagers followed, after which all had a good hearty laugh at them. The villagers, who all went away enjoying the joke as much as we did when they found they had been hoaxed, but the butcher and his wife never lost the name of 'the scared couple'. We remained for an early dinner and then made our way home to London.[187]

1810

June passed on, and Mr Arnold commenced his second season, which consisted of operas, of course. *The Commissioner* M. P. King brought out, Addison *The Siege of Smolensko* and Monk Lewis, as he was called,[188] *One o'Clock*.[189] I was cast into a very bad part, and began to show my consequence by not playing it. However, a few nights afterward, I was asked to play the principal part in consequence of Mr Philip being taken ill.[190] About this time the

---

[187] Such pranks apparently were a speciality of Mathews. For another instance, see Kelly, *Reminiscences, op. cit.*, p 332.

[188] See note 175 on page 40 above.

[189] *One o'Clock* opened at the Lyceum on 1 August 1811.

[190] Presumably the tenor Thomas Phillips.

proprietors of Drury Lane and Covent Garden determined about rebuilding, and the theatre was soon ready. Inasmuch as we were all offered engagement for Drury Lane season I accepted one also, but not knowing how to act regarding my salary, nor considering the difference between a novice and one acknowledged as a favourite, I said, when asked about terms, 'Oh, I suppose the same will do', but soon found my mistake.

The new Drury Lane opened with *Hamlet*; the second night was *The Duenna*, Sheridan's comic opera. When, upon its repetition, Mr Pyne[191] was engaged to play Antonio—always considered the second part—while I, who had chosen the part of Ferdinand at the English Opera House because it was a good acting part,[192] and not being afraid of a rival in a Mr Marshall, an elderly gentleman,[193] soon found that in Mr Pyne I might meet with one who, if he did not take the best parts away, he would stand in my way as a singer, for he had a good voice, had been a favourite in a minor theatre and, of course, his friends would support him as they did on the first night of his appearance, for the applause he received on his entrance coming on to me surprised and mortified me for the moment.

This was the first jealous feeling I had of anyone, and this made me turn to writing, for I thought, well, he knows nothing of music and I can at all events compose. Harry Bishop had the opera of *The Maniac* ready, and I was to have played a part in it, but they feared overcrowding it with music, so the part was arranged for an actor who did not sing.[194] This reminds me that *One o'Clock*, Lewis's opera, was not brought out till after this period, because Pyne was the lover and I [was] cast into a part I refused.

---

[191] James Kendrick Pyne, tenor, 1785–1857.

[192] CEH played Ferdinand in *The Duenna* at the Lyceum Theatre on 22 February 1810.

[193] Probably Thomas Marshall, actor, *d*1819?.

[194] Henry Bishop's *The Maniac, or The Swiss Banditti* opened at the Lyceum on 13 March 1810.

After Bishop's opera of *The Maniac*, I was applied to for the music of a melodrama called *The Magic Bride*.[195] There were a few melodramatic pieces required and a chorus or two. It appeared to give satisfaction, and my ambition was excited so much so that I became nervous and would not even go into the theatre during its performance. The piece was written by that extraordinary character Sir Lumley Skeffington,[196] and the piece was a total failure, and my mortification was intense. I, who thought during the rehearsal that Mozart and Haydn only was my superior and that I should some day be their equal, I was informed by a friend that night of the dreadful fate, that the people hissed and laughed all the way through at what was intended to be most interesting. I shed tears and vowed I would never write for the stage again.

The next morning I was called to a rehearsal and I hid myself in the theatre so as not to be seen by the manager or the author, thinking all the while that my music ought to have been listened to, and [that] the whole failure or success depended upon the music I had written, forgetting that Mrs Edwin, the celebrated beauty,[197] and two or three clever actors had much to do. The morning papers had never condescended to say one word about the music—this was another blow—and I was literally ashamed of being seen to walk through the streets, fearing everybody knew me and would point at me. I found this morning they were cutting the piece, for what I considered [it was] pretty impudent to put it before the public again; and this ceremony was over and not called for.

I was sneaking out of the theatre a[nd] met suddenly Mr Arnold, the proprietor and manager, who called me to step into his room. I thought I was going to get a lecture for all the misfortune of the previous evening. When I came into the room he said, 'Well, Horn, your music was very pretty, but nothing to save the piece. Here is a new farce which I hope will be more successful. At all events you will have some talent to sing your music, for there are parts for Mrs

---

[195] CEH's *The Magic Bride* opened at the Lyceum on 26 December 1810.

[196] Lumley St George Skeffington, playwright and fop, 1771–1850.

[197] Elizabeth Rebecca Edwin, actor and singer, *d*1854.

Mountain, Miss Kelly, Mr Mathews and Lovegrove'.[198] The piece was called *The Bee Hive* (first performed January 19th, 1811);[199] the songs of Mrs Mountain and Miss Kelly all admired and encored.[200]

1811

Mathews's song, 'When a man weds', became a great favourite with the public and was greatly admired for the rapidity of the sounds and the excellent manner in which he sang it. An anecdote here is worth mentioning of the celebrated James Smith, one of the authors of the *Rejected Addresses*.[201] I found in Mathews's songs—for there were two, and so precisely alike that I could not divert myself from writing the songs alike in character—therefore, [I] called on friend Smith, an eminent lawyer, in White Friars, and told him my trouble. We arranged to maintain the original words but adding a line between each, which I left for him to do, and went on to call upon a friend or two in the City. Gauge of my surprise when I came home to dinner to find a letter per post with the song done!! He received the request of mine at 10 in the morning and by 3 o'clock it was at my apartments in Rathbone Place, which reminds me of my first marriage, for here I first lived, having married [on 19 August 1810] the young lady Matilda [Ray] mentioned during my first visit to Cheltenham with Incledon, which all turned out a most unfortunate alliance, and perhaps this circumstance made me forget that which has ever since given me the most acute pain.[202]

---

[198] William Lovegrove, actor and singer, 1778–1816.

[199] At the Lyceum Theatre.

[200] The first performance of *The Bee Hive* is described and reviewed in J. M. Williams (ed.), *The Dramatic Censor ... for the year 1811*, London, 1812, cols. 69–70.

[201] James Smith, solicitor and author, 1775–1839, wrote *Rejected Addresses* (London, 1812) together with his brother Horatio Smith, author, 1779–1849. They were parodies, in the styles of different poets, of addresses composed to commemorate the 10 October 1812 re-opening of Drury Lane Theatre following the fire that destroyed the former theatre on 24 February 1809.

[202] For Matilda Ray see note 90 on page 28 above. CEH and Matilda probably lived at 13 Rathbone Place, as the Cambridgeshire County Record Office,

But an incident occurred at that wedding I have ever remembered and, for the benefit of others, here relate it. I had courted a beautiful, amicable and accomplished young lady, obtained the sanction of our parents, and my mother and sister Henrietta were present, having gone down to Prittlewell near Southend[203] a day or two before, to where Miss — [i.e., Miss Matilda Ray] and her sister[204] were staying.[205] I came down the day before and we all arranged at night to meet at the church at 8 o'clock, I having to remain at my hotel. On my way across the fields, the sun shining brightly on the 19th of August, I set me down on a stile reflecting on my future fate, what might be, when I heard 4 bells of a distant church announce a wedding was to take place. At that sound, I started. My heart (be not surprised, friend reader) sung within me, a still came over me, and I would have given a thousand pounds to have got off my engagement. And, with difficulty, I roused myself and began my walk towards the church.

I espied my friends at the distance, and the sight of the beautiful face of my future bride[206] for a time drove away all

---

Huntingdon has a 25 January 1811 letter written from that address by her father, Edward Ray, to 'Sir'. I am grateful to Peter Ray for information about this letter.

[203] In Essex.

[204] Harriott Ray, baptised 20 September 1789.

[205] According to 'Memoir of C. E. Horn', *Oxberry's Dramatic Biography*, v 6 (1826) p 3–11, at p 6 (which mistakenly states that CEH's marriage took place on 19 August 1811), 'Mr Horn was a most attentive and impassioned lover. During a great part of the time, Miss Ray was attached to a theatre, at one of our fashionable watering-places [Southend], where it was a certain sight to behold of a Sunday morning Charles Horn upon the top of the London stage[coach], having contrived to get out of Saturday night's performance in the metropolis, to spend a few extatic [sic] hours with her'.

[206] Matilda Horn's beauty was widely recognised. For instance, in December 1815, in a scene from *The Merchant of Bruges* that Joseph Shepherd Munden, actor, 1758–1832, played with her at Drury Lane Theatre, 'he exclaimed, pointing to Mrs Horn, ... "Is she not beautiful?", [and] the audience acknowledged the justness of the allusion by a round of applause' ([Thomas Shepherd Munden], *Memoirs of Joseph Shepherd Munden, Comedian, by his Son*, London, 1846, p 249). See also 'Memoir of Mrs C. Horn', *Oxberry's Dramatic Biography, op. cit.*

melancholy thoughts and, after a ceremonious introduction to the clergyman, we all made for the church. My poor mother cried as much as if it was a daughter she was going to lose instead of getting rid of one of the four sons she had and, in her confusion, she put the clergyman's spectacles in her pocket in place of her own while signing the register, which produced a laugh from us all.[207] And, after all was settled, we started in 2 carriages to breakfast 12 miles off, I forget the town. A son [Charles Horn] was the consequence of this marriage, who was born 20 May 1811.

Mathews came during my composing his songs for *The Bee Hive* and would walk about the room, singing, and using a long whip I had at the time. My reputation as a composer took root from the effect of this music, for—although it was nothing extraordinary—yet Mrs Mountain's bravura, which contained an obligato oboe part for Mr Heavy, brought him and me into notice, he particularly with the audience, for Mathews generally introduced a joke of his own, playing an innkeeper's part who was [a] cook also. He recommended oboes with Heavy's sauce for one of his dishes.

About this time *The Beggar's Opera* had been revived for Mr T[om] Phillips to appear as Captain Macheath and, this being a great favorite part of Incledon, he met me one day in Bow Street, Covent Garden. Incledon—being very conceited and jealous of anybody playing a part he has distinguished himself in—said to me (in the presence of Jack Johnstone the Irishman, H. Thomson, and [Joseph Shepherd] Munden), 'Charles, my dear boy, Tom Phillips is making a big bore of himself; you should have played Macheath, as you have seen me play the part oftener than any man'. We laughed and complimented his personation of that gentleman footpad!!

After the success [of] *The Bee Hive*, S[amuel] Beazley's farce of *The Boarding House* [was] my next essay, and came out August

---

[207] This register is preserved at the Essex Record Office, Chelmsford, D/P 183/1/41, and confirms that that CEH's marriage was solemnised in the presence of Diana Horn and Harriott Ray. Matilda Ray, who was engaged by the Southend theatre at this time (see 'Memoir of Mrs C. Horn', *Oxberry's Dramatic Biography*, *op. cit.*, p 20), is described on her marriage record as 'of the parish of Prittlewell'. I am grateful to Colin Gowing for obtaining a copy of this record.

26th.[208] An opera called *Tricks upon Travellers* by Sir James B[land] Burges,[209] in which the well-known composer [William] Reeve wrote the light and I the serious music, also made its appearance,[210] so that I had composed two farces and part of a light opera the first year of my being commenced as a public composer.

I now left my apartments in Rathbone Place and again joined my father at 25 Queen Square, in consequence of my sister's marriage [on 20 April 1811] with my old schoolfellow J[ohn Thomas] Gibson,[211] then a lieutenant only in the Indian Army, and then leaving with Major Gibson for Madras,[212] for they had [had] residence at my father's house. It was here our son Charles was christened.[213]

1812

The person[s] who honoured me with their company were chiefly my father's and my old friends as well as new: Col. Macleod of Colbecks, his lady and two daughters;[214] our friends the Simpsons;

---

[208] CEH's *The Boarding House, or Five Hours at Brighton* opened at the Lyceum on 26 August 1811 and was reviewed in *The Dramatic Censor, op. cit.,* cols. 353–355. Samuel Beazley, architect and playwright, 1786–1851, was the author.

[209] Politician and dramatist, 1752–1824, *later* Sir James Lamb.

[210] CEH's and William Reeve's *Tricks upon Travellers* opened at the Lyceum on 9 July 1810.

[211] See note 57 above. Henrietta Horn's marriage to John Thomas Gibson took place, by licence, at St George the Martyr, Queen Square. I am grateful to Colin Gowing for locating their marriage certificate, which CFH signed on that day.

[212] John Thomas Gibson had become a lieutenant on 20 July 1801. He was promoted to captain on 11 April 1815 and to major on 1 May 1824. See Edward Dodwell and James Samuel Miles, *Alphabetical List of the Officers of the Indian Army from the Year 1760 ... to September 30, 1837*, London, 1838, p 70-71.

[213] I thank Colin Gowing for the information that the baptismal register of St George the Martyr, Queen Square, shows that 'Charles son of Charles Edward and Matilda Horn' was baptised there on 5 May 1812.

[214] Presumably the eldest two of the three surviving daughters of John and Jane (or Jean) Macleod: Georgiana Tweedale Macleod (1798–1818) and Charlotte Carolina Macleod (*b*1799), according to Morrison, *The Macleods, op. cit.,* p 16,

Braham and [Nancy] Storace; Misses Bolton,[215] afterwards Lady Thurlow;[216] Sir George Smart; I. Pocock, the author;[217] Mr Rowlatt and family; Mr E[dward] Stephenson, the banker; Major Stenson;[218] [the] son of the Duke of Norfolk;[219] and many others, in numbers nearly 100 persons after the christening, at which a curious circumstance took place.

Mrs Rowlatt, who had been an old flame of mine, had promised to be the Lady Sponsor or godmother of my son, provided she was to name the child, and I was not to know what it would be called.[220] But he had, in consequence of having been half-baptised at St Giles Church,[221] it was found that the one name he then bore, which was

---

and IGI.

[215] Eliza Bolton, singer, and her sister Mary Catherine Bolton, singer, *c*1790–1830. Both sisters had sung with CEH in Mozart's *Don Giovanni* at Thomas Hayward's floor-cloth manufactory (see King, *Musical Pursuits, op. cit.*, p 145).

[216] On 13 November 1813 Mary Catherine Bolton married Edward Thurlow *later* Hovell-Thurlow, poet, 2nd Baron Thurlow, 1781–1829.

[217] Isaac Pocock, dramatist and painter, 1782–1835. His portrait of CEH, exhibited at the Royal Academy in 1817, is reproduced as the frontispiece to this book.

[218] CEH's spelling of the major's surname is unclear.

[219] The son was Henry Charles Howard (1791–1856, from 1842 13th Duke of Norfolk); he was the only child of Bernard Edward Howard, 1765–1842, from 1815 12th Duke of Norfolk). The son's acquaintance with the Horns perhaps has some connection to the circumstance that he would marry in 1814 Charlotte Leveson-Gower (1788–1870), granddaughter of Granville Leveson-Gower (1721–1803) for whom CFH and Diana Horn had both worked.

[220] Conjecturally she may have been Martha Kilsby, who married William Rowlett at St George Bloomsbury in 1809 (according to Pallot's marriage index). William Rowlett & Co., merchants, are listed at 6 Warnford Court in *Kent's Original London Directory* (London, 1817).

[221] Charles Horn's entry in the baptismal register of St George the Martyr includes the comment: '20th May 1811 Born. Said to be Baptized 21st June 1811.' Presumably the half-baptism mentioned by CEH refers to that June 1811 event. I am grateful to Mark Hodgin, verger of St Giles-in-the-Fields church, which is near Rathbone Place, for the information that no record of Charles Horn's baptism appears in the register of that church, and for advising that it was likely that no entry would have been made in the register if the officiating clergyman was not satisfied that baptism had occurred.

Charles, could not be either altered or added to, so the name Mrs Rowlatt gave, which was 'Charles Mozart', was objected to and, after some explanation from the clergyman, the christening proceeded.[222] After church, dancing and laughter till 4 o'clock in the morning, two violins and a harp was the band, and the whole went off with considerable satisfaction. Would that all which occurred afterwards had been so, but the sequel of this, history will tell.

Mr E[dward] Ray,[223] father of my wife, and family were the same I had met in Cheltenham some years ago and, having been theatrical, and my having chose[n] that profession as a vocalist, and [my] being united to a lady also of the same, caused my father, although courteous, never to feel that I had done myself any honour, when I might have found a partner among my own pupils of family and fortune, and his conduct appeared estranged. We all lived together and, as families have very rarely succeeded in this experiment, whether the house rent and taxes were too heavy, or any other miscalculation or misfortune I know not; from that time our troubles began. My father took a smaller house and I another.

I continued writing and my duties at the theatre. The night after the christening, May 6th, *The Devil's Bridge* came out: I had written part of the music and Braham his songs for the part he played, Count Belino.[224] I sat as conductor, and here relate a curious circumstance to show how we must be guided by public taste if we wish to become popular—or make money. In the song 'Is there a heart that never loved?', there were four more bars, besides those now published, at the close, but the public giving a round of applause at the first close, Braham very adroitly stopped and turned up the stage. I took up the symphony and he did the same, second verse. The song was thus cut

---

[222] CEH seems to be explaining why his son was given no middle name.

[223] Edward Adam Ray was baptised on 5 January 1766 at St Katherine by the Tower church. I am grateful to Peter Ray for this information.

[224] *The Devil's Bridge* opened at the Lyceum on 6 May 1812. The playbills reported that the music was 'composed by Mr Braham and Mr Horn; the overture by Mr Horn'. CFH and CEH presumably moved to their new London residences after then, as the christening party took place at 25 Queen Square.

and stamped by the public and has ever remained so, the great favourite and popular positions it even now holds.

Young Rovedino[225] made his first appearance in this opera on the same night. Mr Arnold, the proprietor, was the author. Braham got 600 pounds for his 6 songs and I, 150 [pounds] for the overture, chorus and concerted music. Mrs Dickons[226] was the Rosalvina, and her songs—of the bravura kind—admired if not encored. Braham's ballads outstopped everything, and *The Devil's Bridge*, with the aid of gunpowder was blow[n] up nightly and occasionally by the papers in the morning, so between the two it was blown and sung into a reputation—it never deserving its popularity.

The next operatic labour of mine was a light one, for it was an opera with more dialogue than music, a species of entertainment the managers liked, because music as it should be done was expensive and not understood by these leaders of the public taste. So I was directed by the manager to see Mr Matthew Lewis or Monk Lewis (so called on account of writing a romance of great notoriety called *The Monk*) as he was called, about the arrangements for the musical play. The name of this bastardised piece of murder was called *Rich and Poor*, altered from one of his own plays called *The East Indian*.[227] Miss F[rances Maria] Kelly was the heroine. Mr [John] Fawcett [Jr performed]. I had the honour of playing a gentleman-villain in Col. Beauchamp.[228] Miss K[elly] and Mr F[awcett] were great in their several parts, and this performance had a run.

---

[225] Presumably Tommasso Rovedino, singer, 1789–1860, as 'Old Rovedino' would have referred to Carlo Rovedino, Italian bass singer, 1751–1822.

[226] Martha (*called* Maria) Poole Dickons, singer and composer, 1774–1833.

[227] *Rich and Poor*, the music of which was 'composed and selected' by CEH, opened at the Lyceum on 22 July 1812. One of the compositions 'selected' by CEH was a fugue from J. S. Bach's '48'—see note 241 below—although, in the music of *Rich and Poor* published by James Power (1766–1836) in London, Bach is not identified as the fugue's composer.

[228] An engraving of CEH playing Beauchamp is reproduced between pages 22 and 23.

1813

About this time I had a most extraordinary connection of the first class of society. For the day on which the Emperor of Russia, the King of Prussia, Blücher and all the ambassadors arrived in London from the Continent,[229] we dined at The Honourable Mr and Mrs Arbuthnot's, and [it] was [a] delightful quiet party in Grosvenor Square,[230] the ladies splendidly dressed as was also my wife, and I thought too much so for my station in life or for my funds in my pocket. However, with a little address, all went off well. During the visit of these monarchs and their representatives, parties were going on in London through the whole summer and autumn,[231] among them was one given by Mr and Mrs Langdon in Harley Street.

My visits also were frequent at Pitt Place, Epsom, belonging to Mr [Thomas] Jeudwine,[232] where I met Lord Coleraine late Col.

---

[229] Although CEH describes this event under the heading '1813', Alexander I (1777–1825, Tsar of Russia), Frederick William III (1770–1840, King of Prussia), and Marshal Gebhard Leberecht Blücher von Wahlstatt (1742–1819) in fact arrived in London on 7 June 1814.

[230] CEH's reference presumably is to the Rt Hon. Charles Arbuthnot, 1767–1850, from 1809 to 1816 Joint Secretary of the Treasury, and to his second wife Harriet Fane Arbuthnot, 1793–1834, whom he married on 31 January 1814. As their London residence in 1814 was at 12 Downing Street, CEH's reference to Grosvenor Square appears to be mistaken; no 'Honourable Mr and Mrs Arbuthnot' have been identified who lived in Grosvenor Square at this time. I am grateful to Andrew Wiseman of Kings College library, University of Aberdeen, for examining Charles Arbuthnot's papers there (Ms 3029) to confirm his London address. In *Wellington and the Arbuthnots: A Triangular Friendship*, London, 1994, p 94, E. A. Smith noted that 'Harriet loved music, the theatre, and the opera and even more the brilliance and conversation of the *salons*, parties, balls and receptions'.

[231] The Prince Regent declared a grand jubilee in 1814 to celebrate the recent victory over Napoléon Bonaparte (1769–1821) and the centennial of Hanoverian rule. Events in London during this season included Queen Charlotte's official welcome of the Duke of Wellington (Arthur Wesley *later* Wellesley, 1769–1852) on his triumphal return to England and a re-enactment of the battle of Trafalgar.

[232] Thomas Jeudwine sold Pitt Place at auction on 11 August 1817. I am grateful to Heidi Lutzeier of the Surrey History Centre for this information.

Hanger[233] and many *bon vivants*. I had made their acquaintances some time before this,[234] when all was high and dried, wine and women and women and wine; but now, as a married man, I had to give up. This was the house that Lord Lyttleton died in, on being warned by an apparition as said![235]

1814

I brought out now a melodrama called *The Woodman's Hut*— April 12.[236] My father came to see its first representation and, finding the wood all on fire, as most magnificently represented at Drury Lane, whether it was fear or discontent, he cried out to me from the front of the house, 'You are all boys and will burn the whole building down'.

Nov[ember] 1st: French importations were daily arriving. Among them was one called *Jean de Paris*,[237] but it was so mutilated by the taste or necessities of the manager that they were obliged to make the French cook or landlord an Irishman for Jack Johnstone (as he was called),[238] who was engaged but had nothing to do. For already English comedy was falling into the Yellow Fear.[239]

---

[233] George Hanger, soldier, 1751?–1824, fourth Baron Coleraine of the second creation. Earlier he was a drinking companion of the Prince of Wales; see Steven Parissien, *George IV: The Grand Entertainment*, London, 2001, p 36–41.

[234] In addition to Pitt Place, *Boyle's Court and Country Guide ... for January, 1812* lists 5 Cleveland Court, St James's Place, London, as a residence of Jeudwine.

[235] Thomas Lyttleton, second Baron Lyttleton, 1744–1779, who was warned of his imminent death in a dream. Jeudwine wrote a letter to the editor of the *Gentleman's Magazine* about this incident ('T.J.' to 'Mr Urban', 6 January 1816, *Gentleman's Magazine* v 86 part 2 (November 1816) p 421–422).

[236] CEH's *The Woodman's Hut* opened at Drury Lane on 12 April 1814.

[237] *Jean de Paris*, by the French composer François Adrien Boieldieu, 1775–1834, was first performed in Paris in 1812 and opened at Drury Lane on 1 November 1814 with music by CEH. He later arranged a 'favourite divertimento' from this opera for the piano. A different English version, *John of Paris*, opened at Covent Garden on 8 November 1814.

[238] See note 184 on page 42 above.

[239] CEH may be indicating that the English were becoming jealous of French

Matilda Horn as Rosalie Somers in *Town and Country (by permission
of the Harry Ransom Humanities Research Center, University of
Texas at Austin)*

Extract of Charles Edward Horn's 10 December 18[24?] letter to Messrs Sainsbury and Co. *(by permission of Jamie and Michael Kassler)*

Nov[ember] 29th: another bastardised melodrama called *The Ninth Statue* came out[240] and I had to compose, again, melodramatic music and [to] re-compose some Irish songs for Johnstone. So old and great a favourite was Johnstone that every farce to be brought out must have an Irishman in it—as in Baghdad, Persia or France, wherever the scene was, an Irishman was the principal feature—so that N° 1 in the French opera *Jean de Paris*, the comic Pedrigo Potts was an Irishman. In *The Ninth Statue* the part to make people laugh was given to an Irishman.

All these things I had to cook up about the time I became a devoted admirer of Sebastian Bach,[241] and although so immersed in putting together those vulgar extravagances for the theatre, wherein the writer of the piece thought he knew more about the music that was to be written than the composer. Indeed, my friend S[amuel] Beazley, the architect and farce-writer, always told me he wrote his songs to one tune, whether comic or serious, so M[atthew] Lewis had always some melodies he wanted to introduce. The same with Skeffington and others. This would annoy me very much. Still, I had to submit in this way. Harry Bishop, now Sir Henry,[242] had to adapt his style and write so hurriedly that he had not time to exercise his well know[n] talent with justice to himself.

---

theatre at this time.

[240] CEH's *The Ninth Statue, or The Irishman in Bagdad* opened at Drury Lane on 29 November 1814.

[241] CFH was a pioneer in introducing the music of Johann Sebastian Bach (1685–1750) to England. In 1807 he published an arrangement of 12 Bach fugues for string quartet, in 1809–1811 he published with Samuel Wesley their adaptation for the piano of six Bach organ sonatas, and in 1810–1813 he and Wesley published their edition of Bach's '48'. CEH subscribed to the latter edition (his name appears on the subscription list as 'Mr Horn Junr'), and in 1812 he included, in the opera *Rich and Poor*, Bach's E♭ major fugue from part 2 of the '48' (BWV 876/2). CEH also composed original music for this opera upon the subject of this fugue.

[242] Bishop was knighted in 1842.

1815

This year I had to prepare another musical farce called *Poor Relations* by Millingen,[243] then my friend, who [had] introduced me as a composer by his musical farce of *The Bee Hive*.

June 15: *Charles The Bold* came out, in which I introduced a great deal of Mozart's composition.[244] It was a very interesting melodrama. Jamie Wallack[245] was the hero and, to show his musical ear—although he knew not a note, or could scarcely turn a tune—he want[ed] a long and spirit[ed] piece of music to represent, as a woodcutter sawing treats kindling for the evening, and [in] a variety of spirited and interesting positions and situation[s]. I took the whole of Mozart['s] Symphony in C called *Jupiter* and, to my astonishment, he put appropriate action to it, and requested no assistance in reminding him how the music and action were to go together. Again, in the scene where the robber came through a large window and prowled about in silence for their booty and victims, I took the slow movement in the E♭ Symphony, in which he was equally successful.

On the closing of the season, Mr Elliston, who had taken the Olympic [Theatre],[246] applied to me to set to music *The Maid and Magpie*.[247] Rossini's celebrated opera not being much known, I question if it was composed [then],[248] as it was taken from the French melodrama.[249] This I consented to do and, being a small theatre and

---

[243] John Gideon Millingen, writer and physician, 1782–1862.

[244] CEH's *Charles the Bold, or The Siege of Nantz* opened at Drury Lane on 15 June 1815.

[245] James William Wallack, actor and (later) theatre manager, 1795–1864.

[246] Robert William Elliston, actor and theatre manager, 1774–1831. He operated the Olympic Theatre from December 1813 until its sale in June 1820.

[247] A melodrama by Thomas John Dibdin, playwright and actor, 1771–1841, that had opened at Drury Lane on 15 September 1815 with music by Henry Bishop.

[248] The opera *La gazza ladra* by Gioachino Rossini, Italian composer, 1792–1868, in fact was first performed in Milan on 31 May 1817.

[249] Both Dibdin's play and the libretto for Rossini's opera were taken from the melodrama *La pie voleuse, ou la servante de Palaiseau* by Louis-Charles Caigniez, 1762–1842, which was first performed at Paris on 29 April 1815.

little to write, I engaged to do for 30 pounds, and for which I had to see him, and pay 10£ to himself. He paid me two or 3^d years afterwards.[250]

I had for some time sang very little—in short had given up my situation as vocalist, and only occupied my time in writing and practising my voice, which my father's old pupil Thomas Welsh[251] persuaded me, that with practice and a little encouragement from him, which he was kind enough to call by that name, although by lessons, and friendly attention, I gained more knowledge, more experience, and [more] reputation as a singer than ever before. Many professors called him a humbug, but if he made a fortune for Miss Stephens, now the Countess of Essex,[252] Miss Shirreff,[253] Mr Sinclair,[254] Miss Wilson, who[m] he afterwards married:[255] with all the good he did, I set down that his knowledge and honesty were far beyond his teaching.

He could not, nor would, take the teaching of notes: sight singing. Consequently, his pupils were generally those for [the] public or who already had knowledge of music. His art was the development and power of the voice, whether it was nature, voice of falsett[o], *vocae de petto*, or *vocae de testa*.[256] Then again, his

---

[250] Besides CEH and Bishop, Henry Smart also composed music for a translation of Caigniez's *La pie voleuse* that opened at the Lyceum on 21 August 1815.

[251] Bass singer, teacher and composer, 1770–1848. In 1825, Welsh and William Hawes (composer, teacher and music director, 1785–1846) became joint proprietors of the music-publishing business that previously called itself the Royal Harmonic Institution. A Welsh and Hawes catalogue printed about May 1826 on the back of their publication of CEH's song 'I've been roaming' advertises that they published more than 20 works by CEH.

[252] Catherine Stephens, soprano and actor, 1794–1882, married George Capell, 5th Earl of Essex, on 19 April 1838.

[253] Jane Shirreff, soprano, 1811–1883.

[254] John Sinclair, tenor, 1790–1857.

[255] Mary Anne Wilson, soprano, 1802–1867. She married Thomas Welsh on 9 June 1827.

[256] Chest tone or head tone.

expression was refined and alway carried with it good sense. This instruction I got from him was quizzed by the press, and one called me 'Master Horn in leading-strings'.[257] The profession laughed, and I with them, and I replied 'let none laugh that man', for I had never been able to get about 8 pounds a week; and now when, Mr Arnold hearing me, I was engaged at 14, 15 and 16 pounds a week for the English Opera House season, and the same terms and time for Drury Lane Theatre.

I was now preparing a character or two for my appearance and [i.e., at] the English Opera House, and Miss Merry, afterwards Mrs Hunt, was practising.[258] She was a young lady with a most exquisite voice of a full clarinet tone, with execution full, rich and articulate; so much so that, in singing the passages of 'Rejoice greatly',[259] I did not know which was the most brilliant: her vocal execution, of [i.e., or] her instructor's piano playing—and all singers know the difficulty of them [the passages] If they do not I would advise them to look at them and practise them daily. Indeed, I have always considered Handel's song the finest practice for a student. Indeed, if the pupil has a good pronunciation of the open vowels, I would always lure them with the study of solfeggio.

Well, to return to my own progress. Miss Merry and myself were to appear in *Artaxerxes*,[260] she as Mandane and I as Artabanes. I proposed to appear in another character without injuring my partner's prospects in appearing as a prima donna in that arduous part, Mandane. Therefore it was arranged I should appear first in a character I should have more chance in, and this was The Seraskier[261] in [Stephen] Storace's opera *The Siege of Belgrade*. I sang for the first

---

[257] Leading-strings were used to support a child learning to walk; the implication is that CEH was still a pupil who had much to learn from Welsh.

[258] Lydia Ellen Merry, who married Henry Hunt in 1818 (Pallot's marriage index).

[259] 'Rejoice greatly, o daughter of Zion', from Handel's *Messiah*.

[260] By Thomas Augustine Arne, composer, 1710–1778.

[261] i.e., the commander-in-chief of the Turkish army.

time at rehearsal, and Miss [Frances] Kelly was the Lilla and her sister Lydia,[262] Katherine.[263]

But, before we come to my appearance, I should explain. The E[nglish] Opera House had been burnt down, the one [in which] I first appeared in 1809, and Mr Arnold found upon rebuilding the new one and applying for his licence—the theatre being ready to make all preparations for opening—he could not get it, and was told His Majesty's indisposition, which had taken place in the meantime, that nothing could be done about it, no licences for public amusements could be delicately applied for. Upon thus hearing, Welsh said to me one day, could you see to speak with the Queen. I said I did not know—my father had been so little to Windsor or the palace[264]—but I could see H. R. H. The Princess Augusta, who was a great favourite with her mother. So we agreed to try the experiment by going down together to Windsor.

I got instructed now by Welsh in diplomatic affairs. We arrived about six, went to a hotel, found that the best hour to see the princess was when she left the dinner table, before she returned to the Queen for the evening. This was to be about ½ 7 or 8. I boldly found her apartments in the quadrangle at that time, and rang, asked one of the servants if I could [see] Princess Augusta's page, who was immediately called to me. I told me name, which was remembered through my father's situation as instructor, and I was obliged to tell this page what I wanted, for sometimes it is politic to make the hireling interested in your business. And I succeeded so well that this person became quite as interested as myself, who had a 3 years engagement upon a rising salary. He told me to wait in the anteroom

---

[262] Lydia Eliza Kelly, singer, *b*1795.

[263] CEH's return to the stage, performing The Seraskier at the Lyceum Theatre, took place on 1 July 1816. *The Theatrical Inquisitor and Monthly Mirror for July 1816* reported (p 67) that his voice, which 'was extremely feeble' when he had last performed, was now 'increased wonderfully in strength and compass'. His acting also was 'considerably improved'. The anonymous reviewer predicted that CEH would 'hold a foremost rank among our vocal performers'.

[264] CFH's instruction of the Royal Princesses had ended in October 1812 (Royal Archives).

and the moment H. R. Highness left the table he would say who wished to see her.

We met, but it was not in a crowd, and I therefore had a full chance of explaining all: that the Theatre was built on the faith, word and patronage of His Majesty granting the licence originally, and that the engagements of nearly 200 persons depended on its proceeding. Besides that, Mr Arnold had expended a very large sum upon the building and its success. Princess Augusta said, I will mention this in less than an hour, so if you will come here by 7 o'clock in the morning I will give you an answer. Welsh and I spent the evening, by going to see Dr Herschel's telescope at Datchet, and had a long conversation with the old astrologist.[265]

The next morning I saw H. R. Highness, who said H[er] Majesty graciously was pleased to say that the King's word and promise must be kept a[s] sacred as his name, and that if I went to the Lodge at 9 o'clock Gen[l] Taylor[266] would explain to me how to proceed. I met the gallant soldier, who said, 'Ah, Mr Horn, I've heard you often and we know your songs. We shall have an English Opera in spite of all. You must desire Mr Arnold to draw a memorial to Her Majesty and the Queen will sanction it. Get it done immediately under cover to me and send it through the Horse Guards.'

I thanked him and went to Welsh. We congratulated each other, walked about the [Windsor] Park, came off by the 2 o'clock coach, returned to Town, and called on Mr Arnold who was seated at his dinner table with Mrs Arnold.[267] He look[ed] very down and said, 'what brought you two here?'. Welsh said, 'ask Horn'.

So I began by saying (for the cloth was drawn, but there were no signs of glasses) 'if you give us a glass of wine, I'll tell you'. He smiled and told his servant to bring wine, when I commenced, 'how

---

[265] Sir William Herschel, astronomer and musician, 1738–1822, had lived in Datchet from 1782 to 1785, but moved to Slough in April 1786. In 1815, therefore, CEH and Thomas Welsh presumably visited Herschel in Slough.

[266] General Sir Herbert Taylor, secretary to King George III and Queen Charlotte, 1775–1839.

[267] Samuel James Arnold had married Matilda Caroline Pye (1772?–1851) in 1802.

gets on the Theatre?'. He shook his head and looked sad, and said 'I am a ruined man'. When I replied, 'No, you are not, if you alluded to the opening of the House, for Welsh and I have been to Windsor. I saw Princess Augusta; your case was laid before the Queen last night—and—I have her command to tell you to memorialise her— and she will sanction.'

He jumped, shook hands, thanked us, brought some wine, sent for his treasurer, Richard Peake,[268] and, after giving all particulars of my proceedings at Windsor, dispatched the memoir, and Mr Arnold said, 'I'll give you a share in the concern'. But he never did.

Well, the House opened at its promised time. Another singer or two had to make an appearance. When my name was announced as a young gentleman to make his appearance in The Seraskier, it soon got blazed about who it was; and my name was announced with some newspaper confidential remarks that a great alteration and improvement had been elicited through the agency of Thomas Welsh, so that the public had to expect something.

The night came and I was encored in four songs: 'The rose and the lily', 'My heart with love is beating', 'The serenade', and 'The Austrian trumpet's bold alarm', the duetto and Braham's quartetto. This was pronounced a triumph.

After a week or two, during which I had appeared every night, *Artaxerxes* came on and Miss Merry appeared.[269] However, whether from nervousness or anything else I know not, she did not satisfy Mr Welsh, and she looked so melancholy and wretched that I am sure it was the chief cause of her failure. The first night she was joined for the opening duet she said to me, 'Here's a profession of foolery to get one's bread by'. This convinced me she would never be a favourite— and it was [so].

We got through the season. I was employed through the season and occasionally was invited to the great tragedian, Mrs Siddons, who read to me often and, strange to say, gave me two or three hints in playing Capⁿ Macheath, particularly his comic bits, which gave me

---

[268] 1757–1829, treasurer of Drury Lane Theatre.

[269] Miss Merry's debut as Mandane in *Artaxerxes* took place on 13 July 1816 (*The Theatrical Inquisitor and Monthly Mirror for July 1816*, p 67).

quite a reputation for playing the part. I played Belino[270] and in a new opera called *The Election* by J[oanna] Baillie,[271] in which I wrote the song, 'Love in the heart'.[272]

1815 and 1816

At Drury Lane we—Miss Merry and self—appeared in the same parts. Afterwards a Miss Mangeon[273] made her appearance in *Lionel and Clarissa*,[274] and I was cast as Lionel, but which Mr Welsh took so much to heart that I refused the part, made myself enemies with the managers, and was never treated with confidence. They revived an opera called *Wine does Wonders* but which did no wonders for the treasury: everybody was put on it.[275] Notwithstanding the whole of the vocal strength, and [i.e., as] well as Coveney,[276] Munden and Johnstone, it failed. I was given a[n] Indian's part, [the] part [of] Zemaun, with introduced songs, and they did well.[277] Poor

---

[270] In *The Devil's Bridge*.

[271] Scottish playwright, 1762–1851.

[272] CEH's *The Election* opened at the Lyceum on 7 June 1817.

[273] According to a report in the April 1817 number of *La Belle Assemblée*, Miss Mangeon, daughter of William Mangeon (c1772–1816) and Elizabeth Mangeon, hoteliers of Clifton near Bristol, was a pupil of Sarah Mountain and made her first appearance at Drury Lane Theatre on 6 December 1816. IGI gives her name as Henrietta Charlotte Lucy Mangeon (b1798). She was a niece of Harriet Mangeon (1796–1863), who married the composer Ferdinand Ries (1784–1838) in 1814. I am grateful to Barbara Mühlens-Molderings for information about the Mangeon family.

[274] By Isaac Bickerstaffe, Irish playwright, 1735–1812.

[275] The revival of *Ramah Droog; or Wine Does Wonders*, the words by James Cobb, 1756–1818, and the music by Joseph Mazzinghi, 1765–1844, and William Reeve, opened at Drury Lane on 18 December 1816. The opera had first been performed on 12 November 1798 at Covent Garden.

[276] CEH's handwriting of this name is not clear. On playbills for *Ramah Droog* at Drury Lane on 18 and 19 December 1816 the name that appears closest to what CEH wrote is 'Mr Coveney', who played the part of an Indian officer. I am grateful to the Theatre Museum, London, for examining their copies of these playbills.

[277] Two 'introduced' songs, composed by CEH, were entered at Stationers' Hall

Miss Merry was ineffective again, and [the] opera season dragged on to the end, I fear with great loss to the Committee, till the Opera House season opened again, when I found Miss Merry had seceded and gave up her engagement.

I, being alone, looked out for some one to sing with me and found [her] in Miss M[iriam] Hammersley, a young girl from the chorus of Drury Lane.[278] She had received lessons from me, and I brought her out in Mandane[279] and Polly [in] *The Beggar's Opera*, with such éclat that she was called the young Billington.[280] It would be but fair [to say] that I derived much information from Mr Welsh and adopted it to my own pupil. I consulted him upon bringing her out, which he did not like, but what was I to do? I could not wait for another of his pupils. They succeeded well, and she and her sister Lavinia gave concerts in the different cities through England.[281] However, they could not return again to Drury Lane as choir singers,

---

on 8 February 1817: 'If maidens would marry—a favorite song, first sung by Mrs Horn, and introduced by Mrs Bland, with the greatest applause, in the opera of *Ramah Droog*, as performed at the Theatre Royal Drury Lane' and 'Turn to this heart—duett sung by Miss Merry and Mr Horn at the Theatre Royal Drury Lane'.

[278] Miriam H. Buggins, who (according to *Oxberry's Dramatic Biography* v 1 (1825) p 147) adopted 'Hammersley' as her stage name after initially appearing in London 'under her real, though *terrible* cognomen of *Buggins*'. She performed as Miss M. H. Buggins with CEH in his opera *The Persian Hunters* which opened at the Lyceum Theatre on 13 August 1817 (see *The Theatrical Inquisitor and Monthly Mirror for November 1817*, p 367–368).

[279] In Arne's *Artaxerxes*.

[280] Mrs Billington had earlier appeared in this opera.

[281] In his letter of about September 1817 to Robert William Elliston (New-York Historical Society), CEH mentioned his plan to perform in October 1817 with 'Miss Miriam H. Buggins' and another 'young lady' pupil, probably her sister, in Leicester and in Birmingham where 'my pupils will have ... the curiosity of their friends'. This latter remark suggests that the Misses Buggins may have been the Miriam and Louisa Buggins baptised at St Phillips, Birmingham, on 16 April 1801 (IGI), whose father, Samuel Buggins, conceivably was the Birmingham musician of that name.

and the committee were a little annoyed that I did not make choice of their House to bring them out.[282]

An operatic drama was brought out called (April 17th) *Elphi Bey*; [it] came out now with Attwood's music.[283] I wrote me song, a bravura for myself, but the libretto was bad and it failed.[284] During all this period my home has become very miserable, and as I appeared to succeed in public estimation my privacy was being undermined, when [CEH's relationship with Matilda] ended to[o] melancholy to enter in any explanation again.

July the 26 I composed the music of an operatic melodram[a] *The Wizard*,[285] taken from W. Scott's *Dwarf*.[286] There are some duetto and trio still noticed by the public. And, being now employed on an opera called *The Persian Hunters*,[287] I had employment enough, for I had 4 tenors besides myself: Broadhurst,[288] L. Lee,[289] J. Jones

---

[282] In 1819 CEH sought to find employment for Miriam Hammersley (as she was then called) at Drury Lane Theatre, stating that she had 'a most prodigious fair voice, good figure, and [was] a very clever actress' (CEH letters to Robert William Elliston, 9 July 1819 and 11 September 1819; to George Robins, 9 July 1819, all at the University of Missouri, Kansas City).

[283] Thomas Attwood's *Elphi Bey, or The Arab's Faith* opened at Drury Lane on 17 April 1817. Attwood 'selected' the overture to this work and some of its 'concerted pieces' from music by Mozart, with whom he had studied.

[284] In addition to music composed and selected by Attwood, *Elphi Bey* included this song by CEH and another song by Henry Smart.

[285] CEH's *The Wizard, or The Brown Man of the Moor* opened at the Lyceum on 26 July 1817.

[286] *The Black Dwarf* by Sir Walter Scott, Scottish novelist, 1771–1832.

[287] CEH's *The Persian Hunters, or The Rose of Gurgistan* opened at the Lyceum on 13 August 1817.

[288] *The Dramatic Censor ...*, op. cit., col. 452, remarked that Broadhurst's voice had the quality of a 'counter-tenor', and stated that his first appearance took place on 21 November 1811 at Covent Garden. He is described in *A Dictionary of Musicians ...*, London, printed for Sainsbury and Co., 1824, v 1 p 116, as 'an English tenor singer of much sweetness, in part songs'. His first name has not been found.

[289] Presumably the singer and (later) music publisher Louis Leoni Lee (*d*>1862).

now in America,[290] and Pearman,[291] besides my own pupil as prima donna. The tenors were jealous of me, for I had 3 songs and two duetto, one with the bass voice, called 'The Tiger Hunt'. And they were sulky, jealous and almost mad, till they heard their songs which were all liked by then and—what was still more strange—all encored. When my own songs fell to the ground they would positively try and push me on the stage to any slight indication of an encore, which singers think so much of in general.

My own affairs at home getting entangled and Mr Jones, Frederick Jones Esq., the manager of Dublin, was in town.[292] He made me an offer: if I could give up my next season at Drury Lane he would guarantee me a larger sum [than] I was receiving in London. In consequence of which I engaged my pupils at Manchester and took an engagement myself in Dublin, in order to get rid of all reflection of London.[293]

A Miss Byrne[294] was engaged as the lady singer, and here I find also Lydia Kelly. I appeared as Young Meadows,[295] and introduced my song 'The ray that beams forever',[296] which I sang nightly, 3 times each night. *The Siege of Belgrade* by Storace, *The Devil's Bridge*,[297] and other operas were got up for me. Sir John Stevenson,[298] Dr Smith,[299] Spray,[300] and James McCaskey with the Beef Steak Club

---

[290] John Jones, tenor, 1796–1861.

[291] William Pearman, tenor, *b*1792.

[292] Frederick Edward Jones, theatre manager, *c*1759–1834. His complex affairs are a subject of Walsh's book *Opera in Dublin, 1798–1820, op. cit.*

[293] CEH and his wife were estranged about this time. See note 93 above.

[294] Mary Byrne, Irish soprano. See Walsh, *op. cit.*, Chapter 9.

[295] In *Love in a Village*.

[296] By Michael Kelly.

[297] Walsh, *Opera in Dublin, op. cit.*, states (p 181) that CEH made his first Dublin appearance as Count Belino in *The Devil's Bridge* on 4 December 1817.

[298] Irish composer, 1761–1833.

[299] John Smith, Mus. Doc., composer and singer, 1797–1861.

[300] John Spray, tenor and composer, *d*1827, uncle of Dr John Smith.

contributed to make my sojourn here very delightful. I soon got a very excellent position of teaching. My first benefit gave me 300 pounds clear of all expense, and I found my change from London was all that I could desire. W. Farren was stage manager,[301] and I was very happy under all circumstances in this theatre.

Money was at times very scarce, and the whole concern mortgaged to Vesey Fitzgerald, brother to the M.P.,[302] and [a] person of great influence.[303] At one time, while Mr Fitzgerald and Mr Jones had some dispute about money matters, and the company not receiving money for some 5 and 6 weeks, notwithstanding there had been some fine houses, I came for my money one Saturday and found the whole company at the door storming the treasury with sighs! For some were without a dinner and, upon inquiry, had like myself been some 5 weeks without. They all told me [that] Mr Fitzgerald, the mortgagee, was there with the treasurer and that he has been desired to say there was no money. I was much surprised at this and said, 'let me in'. I knocked at the door, was let in, and very politely told there was no money. 'How is this? I have never asked for any this long time.'

Upon this Mr F. said, in a strong Irish accent, 'No, Mr Horn, there is no money for the performers', upon which I said, 'I believe you are the mortgagee of this property and I know the performers are first to be paid, and I am ashamed of a man of property like you letting these poor people want a dinner when you know they earned

---

[301] William Farren, actor and theatre manager, 1786–1861. According to the *Dictionary of National Biography* he 'bade farewell' to Dublin on 19 August 1818.

[302] The member of parliament was William Fitzgerald, statesman, c1782–1843, who took the name 'Vesey Fitzgerald' in 1815.

[303] Walsh, *Opera in Dublin, op. cit.,* reports (p 162) that Frederick Jones 'assigned an interest in the Crow Street Theatre property'—the Theatre Royal, Dublin—to Maurice Fitzgerald on 29–30 May 1816. In a deed dated 9 June 1817 and registered on 8 March 1818, Jones's 'right, title and interest in and to one-eighth part of the Theatre Royal and Letters Patent ... formerly assigned in trust to Maurice Fitzgerald Esq.' were conveyed to two other persons (p 194). On 18 May 1820 the *Dublin Evening Post*, according to Walsh p 228, appeared to identify Maurice Fitzgerald as the 'principal creditor' of this theatre.

it. Now, if you don't send me my money by 4 o'clock this day, I will arrest you, Mr Vesey Fitzgerald'. 'You will, will you', said he, 'Do you hear that, Mr Stapleton the treasurer, Mr Horn will arrest Vesey Fitzgerald. You may do as you please, but Mr Vesey Fitzgerald knows his own business better than you can tell him.'

Upon which I left the treasury, made my bow, and told I would do so, not for my own sake so much but to set an example to the others. When I came out, all asked me what hopes would be expected, when I replied that I had left a message the result of which I would explain in the evening. I went about my teaching, and came home at four o'clock to dinner. On my dinner table was left a note with the whole amount of my 5 weeks' salary, which I explained to a few of the performers. For once in my life a straightforward, honest but rough conduct (I will own) was successful, but the example to others lost many of them their situations. Such was the system of theatrical management in the year 18—, and by no means confined to Dublin, for it was the same in London.

My engagement in Dublin was valuable to the managers. In London it was not, for opera was at a discount: no prima donna. So my fuss succeeded, or rather my independence. I was not happy in this event, for I never could bear to do any thing harshly, and I believe it was the conduct towards the inferior part of the company that exasperated me into such determination. I gave some of them a few shillings apiece, principally [the] chorus, and so divided my 5 weeks' salary nearly among them.

In the morning, Sunday, I received a letter at my breakfast table to the following purport: Mr Jones wishes to see Mr Horn very particularly, as early as convenient, Foxgrove, Dublin. Well!!, I thought to myself, here will be a pretty row: Mr Jones, the manager, in [i.e., is] angry by his note. I will go immediately after breakfast, in place of going to the cathedral. I walk[ed] up to his house in tribulation, for I hate getting into misunderstanding, and was framing to myself what excuse I should make to being so blunt, or distressing the concern,[304] when I perceived Mr Jones coming down from the house. When taking hold of my hand, he said, 'Mr Horn, I wish you

---

[304] i.e., distressing the management of the theatre company.

had put that d—d old villain V[esey] Fitzgerald into prison. I am glad you served him as you did, and I hope by the Mighty G[od] above us that the villain will be served the same by every member of the company'.

Although I had be[en] a dramatic singer for 8 or 10 years I was not aware how untheatrically I was behaving. My composition, my teaching was all that I thought of, as everything appeared so vilely conducted. W. Farren looked on, and many other friends were wondering and thinking about the independent manner in which I had behaved, while [I was] quite unconscious that I had done any thing contrary to strict propriety for a man who was singing and placing himself at the disposal of a manager for one year.[305] But the deceit leaked out.

Miss [Catherine] Stephens was expected, and I was engaged to sing with her in Dublin, Cork and Limerick.[306] And, once being a favourite in Dublin, they received me at all other places where I had clear benefits at each place, and Miss S. had to play or sing for me gratis. This altogether rendered me a very greater object to the manager and also gave me a very splendid sum towards my engagements. Miss Stephens arrived at Dublin, and I appeared with her in *Love in a Village*.[307] She of course was greeted with enthusiastic applause. I had my share. I remember her singing Bishop's song 'The mocking bird' which then she sang in F, and her

---

[305] Walsh, *Opera in Dublin, op. cit.*, p 185–189, reports that on 25 May 1818 CEH apologised publicly, in the newspapers and on stage, for failing to appear as advertised in the entertainment *A Minstrel's Summer Ramble* on 23 May, although earlier that evening CEH did appear in *Rob Roy Macgregor; or Auld Lang Syne*, an opera written by Isaac Pocock and John Davy, composer, 1763–1824.

[306] Catherine Stephens and CEH began their Limerick performances on 22 October 1818 (Walsh, *op. cit.*, p 197).

[307] The pasticcio *Love in a Village* opened in Dublin on 25 July 1818, with Catherine Stephens playing Rosetta and CEH playing Young Meadows (Walsh, *op. cit.*, p 195).

going up to F in alt,[308] holding it on the pause. The effect was electrical, but I never heard her do [it] again.[309]

1827

After such a scene of misery,[310] successes and [blank] I was offered an engagement by E. Price, manager and lessee of the N[ew] Y[ork] Park Theatre,[311] and resolved to go.[312] I had engaged to go to

---

[308] i.e., to the F two octaves and a fourth above Middle C.

[309] CEH's memoir breaks off here, without mentioning that, in June 1818, he met and heard Michael William Balfe, Irish composer, singer and violinist, 1808–1870, play in Dublin (Walsh, *op. cit.*, p 191, records that Balfe performed on 5 June 1818 at a benefit concert for CEH and Mrs [Isaac] Willis [née Cheese] at the Rotunda, Dublin). Five years later Balfe went with CEH to London as CEH's apprentice, and later he became a pupil of CFH (see Charles Lamb Kenney, *A Memoir of Michael William Balfe*, London, 1875, p 15–19 and p 33). On 9 July 1819 CEH's address was 87 Dame Street, Dublin (CEH to George Robins, letter of that date, University of Missouri, Kansas City). Matilda Horn apparently remained in London at this time. Her 14 August 1819 letter to James Winston (Folger Shakespeare Library Ms Add 1051) was written from 7 Bath Place, West Square, Lambeth; in this letter she remarked that CEH was 'too far off' to aid her solicitation of employment at Drury Lane Theatre.

[310] At about the same time as his final separation from his wife, CEH ('of No. 67, Judd Street, Brunswick Square ..., music and musical-instrument seller, dealer and chapman') declared himself insolvent on 31 October 1826, and was proclaimed bankrupt in the following month (*London Gazette* no. 18301, 31 October 1826, p 2579, and no. 18304, 10 November 1826, p 2673). James Winston, in his journal entry for 12 November 1826, remarked that CEH's 'domestic misfortunes made him withdraw himself' (Nelson and Cross (eds.), *Drury Lane Journal*, *op. cit.*, p 136). Later, in New York, CEH again became a music seller as well as an importer and publisher of music.

[311] The Park Theatre lessee was Stephen Price (*d*1840), who also was the lessee of Drury Lane Theatre (because of this, New Yorkers called the Park Theatre 'Old Drury'). Price lived in London, and his partner Edmund Shaw Simpson (1784–1848) managed the Park Theatre locally, which may explain why CEH wrote the letter 'E.' before 'Price' (after initially leaving a blank space before 'Price').

[312] On 27 May 1827 James Winston wrote in his diary (Nelson and Cross, *op. cit.*, p 149), 'Horn says he will not be at Drury Lane next season. Price has asked him to go to America'. *The Albion* (New York, 20 October 1827, p 152) reported that CEH 'made his first appearance [at the Park Theatre] on

Vauxhall Gardens to sing at 20 pounds a week—then a great salary—and, at the end of this season, August, I wrote to Paul Bedford[313] to take my passage in the ship *Canada*, Capt. [James] Rogers.[314] And, after taking leave of my dear boy Charles and his cousin Alfred Ray[315] to the Golden Cross, Charing Cross,[316] I put myself on a coach box, and my poor dresser was with me by 6 o'clock to take leave. I was half-inclined to take Charles with me but, being safely disposed of with my father at Windsor Castle, I thought it was a pity to let him lose his time for learning—or education.[317]

Wednesday [17 October 1827] in The Seraskier (*Siege of Belgrade*)'. A brief account of the Park Theatre season that commenced on 3 September 1827 is given in R. Osgood Mason, *Sketches and Impressions Musical, Theatrical, and Social (1799–1885) ... from the After-Dinner Talk of Thomas Goodwin*, New York, 1887, p 210–217. See also George C. Odell, *Annals of the New York Stage, v 3, 1821–1834*, New York, 1928, p 304–305. Besides CEH, Lydia Kelly also appeared as a 'star' during that season.

[313] Bass singer and comedian, 1792?–1871, who performed in the Drury Lane opera company from 1824 to 1833. He wrote in his memoirs that he had expected to play Caspar in Carl Maria von Weber's opera *Der Freischütz* at Drury Lane in 1824 but CEH was chosen 'through chicanery' to play that part instead; however, Bedford got the part in 1826 and performed Caspar in the composer's presence (see Paul Bedford, *Recollections and Wanderings ...*, London, 1864, p 61, 65). CEH's letter to Bedford (not preserved) presumably concerned Drury Lane matters.

[314] CEH wrote the captain's surname as 'Rodgers'. I am grateful to Elaine Miller for informing me that the passenger list for the ship *Canada* shows that CEH arrived in New York from Liverpool on 1 October 1827.

[315] Alfred Gustavus Ray, baptised 7 January 1811. I am grateful to Peter Ray for information about this baptism.

[316] The inn from which CEH left by stagecoach for Liverpool.

[317] Later, on 27 June 1833, CEH's son Charles married Jeannette Prosser at St Nicholas, Brighton. A witness to their marriage, Emily Prosser (*bc*1812), presumably Jeannette's sister, married Theobald Peregrine Monzani (flute maker, *bap*1811, son of Tebaldo Monzani, 1762–1839, flautist, flute maker and music publisher) at St George, Bloomsbury, on 17 December 1833. In 1835 Charles and Jeannette Horn and Theobald Monzani all were in New York City, where (and also elsewhere in America) Charles performed with CEH as a tenor (see Richard A. Montague, *Charles Edward Horn: His Life and Works (1786–1849)*, Ed.D. dissertation, Florida State University, 1959, p 40–42, and William C. Smith and Peter Ward Jones, 'Tebaldo Monzani', *New Grove Dictionary of*

Arriving at Liverpool.[318]

Note.[319] This song I once sang to the author of the words, Dr Wolcot, the celebrated Peter Pindar of George the Third memory.[320] My father introduced me for the purpose particularly, telling me the Dr was always sifting him for anecdotes about the Royal Family but never succeeded. However, upon introducing me—about my song—the Dr began about the Queen, asking if she was not fond of diamonds. Upon [which] my father, forgetting himself, said 'yes' and related Her Majesty wearing a homager covered with them; upon which the Dr laughed heartily and said 'How queer she must look with her tallow, tallow-coloured face', and immediately produced the following, which he wrote down but never published, as he was getting out of fashion:

So behold our vain old Queen
with all the diamonds she could muster
Say Muse what like unto her's seen
A Tallow Candle in a Luster.

However, in justice to the Dr, I should give you the lines that first inspired and charmed me with the idea of setting words to his piece, and I feel it was the best thing I have ever written:

The Daughter of Love
Farewell to the fragrance of Morn
Farewell to the Song of the Grove

Music and Musicians, 2nd edition, London, 2001). A composition by 'Charles Horn Junior' entitled 'Norah McShane. A Ballad' was published for him by CEH in New York in 1841; a copy is in the Library of Congress. Subsequently, Charles Horn returned to England, remarried and died at Hackney on 25 April 1887. I am indebted to Colin Gowing for information about Charles Horn's family.

[318] CEH's memoir ends abruptly here.

[319] This note, added by CEH, relates to his text printed on p 36 above.

[320] 'Peter Pindar' was the pseudonym of John Wolcot, poet, 1738–1819.

I go from my Delia forlorn
I go from the daughter of love.

I was told that I ought not to[321]

---

[321] The remainder of this page is blank.

APPENDIX 1

CHARLES FREDERICK HORN'S LETTER TO THE COMPILER OF THE *BIOGRAPHICAL DICTIONARY OF MUSICIANS* (1823)

October 31st 1823.[1]

Charles Frederick Horn, a native of Germany, came to London in the year 1782 where he was kindly received by his late Excellency the Saxon Ambassedeur Count Brühl,[2] and recommended by him to the late Marquis of Stafford in order to instruct in music the Young Ladys the R^t Honble Ladys Leveson-Gower; he then dedicated his first work, *Six Sonatas for the Piano Forte*, to Lady Charlotte, Her Grace the present Duchess of Beaufort.[3]

In the year 1789 he had the distinguished honour of being recommended by Lady Caroline Waldegrave[4] & Mr Clementi (his

---

[1] This letter, the beginning of which is reproduced facing page 22, is in the Glasgow University Library, Euing collection, R.d. 86/105. It bears numerous crossings-out and emendations by a compiler of *A Dictionary of Musicians, from the Earliest Ages to the Present Time* ..., London, printed for Sainsbury and Co., 1824. The emended account that was printed in the *Dictionary* omits, amongst other details in CFH's letter, the dates of his attendance upon Queen Charlotte. The letter is addressed, by someone other than CFH, to the dictionary's publisher, Mr [John Davis] Sainsbury (*bc*1793), at 11 Bells Buildings, Salisbury Square.

[2] John Maurice *or* Hans Moritz, Count von Brühl, diplomatist, astronomer and amateur musician, 1736–1809, from 1764 ambassador of Saxony.

[3] Charlotte Sophia Leveson-Gower married Henry Charles Fitzroy Somerset, 1766–1835, 6th Duke of Beaufort, on 16 May 1791.

[4] 1765–1831, from 1791 to 1798 Lady of the Bedchamber to the elder

friend) to Her late Majesty The Queen Charlotte to instruct Their Royal highnesses the Princesses until the Year 1811;[5] in the interim he was also commanded to attend twice a week on her Majesty from Oct[br] 20 1789 to October 9th 1793.[6]

M[r] Horn has instructed many familys the Piano Forte & Composed for that Instrument *Sonatas & 12 Themes with Variations with an Accompangment for Flute or Violin*[7] &c. &c.

---

princesses.

[5] According to the Royal Archives Treasurer's Account for Queen Charlotte, CFH was paid £200 per year plus disbursements as music master to T. R. H. the Princesses during the period from 29 June 1789 to 10 October 1812.

[6] No record has been located to indicate that CFH was paid additionally for his attendance upon Queen Charlotte.

[7] CFH's themes and variations, named for the twelve months of the year, are dedicated to the Hon. Georgiana Lady Ponsonby (Frances Anne Georgiana Ponsonby, 1817–1910, daughter of William Francis Spencer Ponsonby, 1787–1855, and Barbara Ashley-Cooper, 1788–1844). Their complex publication history has not been fully sorted out. The Kungliga Musikaliska Akadamiens Stockholm possesses (1) copies of *January* (no plate number) and *March* (plate no. 42), inscribed by CFH to Miss Julia King and Miss Maria King respectively, and entitled 'Themes with Variations, for the Piano Forte' (with no mention of flute or violin), printed and sold by W[illiam] Pinnock at 267 St Clements Church Yard, Strand, where this publisher was located between 1822 and 1826; (2) a copy of *February* (plate no. 40), with a similar title-page but no CFH inscription, except that this work was printed and sold by W. Horn at 6 Greek Street, Soho, an address not included amongst the *c*1817–1836 addresses for CFH's son William James Horn in Humphries and Smith, *Music Publishing in the British Isles, op. cit.* The Bibliothek der Hansestadt Lübeck possesses (3) a copy of *June* with a title-page reading 'Thema [not 'Themes'] with Variations for the Piano Forte, and German Flute (at lib)' [sic], with no publisher's name; the music of this *June* is identical to that of *January* Pinnock's publication, but is printed from different plates. The Staats- und Universitäts-Bibliothek Hamburg possesses (4) a copy of *September*, printed and sold by Garlick & Company at 10 Upper King Street, Bloomsbury, where the firm was located between 1823 and 1825; this copy includes a catalogue for T[homas] Garlick & W. Horn, piano manufacturers and music sellers at that address, listing music for sale by CFH, CEH, Balfe and others.

P. M[8]

M[r] Horn beggs The Compiler will correct the orthography of this Sketch—being not an English but a German—and lickwise alter the stile where it is requisite, or contract it, if too long an account—

---

[8] 'P. M' presumably is CFH's mistake for 'P. S.'.

APPENDIX 2

CHARLES EDWARD HORN'S DRAFT SKETCH OF HIS OWN CAREER (1828)

July 17, 1828

It is somewhere observed by our oldest philosophers that necessity is the mother of invention; and, truly, may I plead for and offer this exordium as an explanation of the purpose and nature of this entertainment.[1] A Dibdin, an Incledon and a Mathews have become celebrated from these necessities and reaped a golden harvest by their labours—the one from anecdote of human nature, the other from an unequalled splendid voice, and the last not least, the 3[d], from a most wonderful and powerful art of mimicry.[2]

I appear before you with none of these inducements, no attempt at anecdote, no splendour of vocal ability, no art of mimicry, nothing but—I flatter [myself]—a knowledge of my profession as a theorist and experience as a vocalist from the great celebrated master[s], Italian and English, in Europe. A slight sketch of my professional career, although not amusing, may serve to give confidence in that part of my audience who visit me for instruction. The remainder may learn how strange is the vicissitudes of life, in whatever situations we are found in.

At an early period of my life I was instructed as a composer and pianoforte teacher by my father (a German by birth), then holding the official situation of Instructor of Music to the present royal family of England. Not relishing the dry study of thorough bass and

---

[1] CEH apparently prepared this autobiographical account for presentation to an American audience that he conceived might include prospective pupils.

[2] CEH appears to be referring to Thomas John Dibdin, Charles Incledon and Charles Mathews.

counterpoint, I soon tried, by continually singing my p[iano]forte lessons, whether I had any chance to derive emolument from my vocal abilities. To my father I am indebted for my studying thorough bass and harmony; and to his perseverance, and not my own. I [am] indebted for any little credit I may have for my compositions and their orchestral arrangements.

Still, singing was my aim and he, not be[ing] able to draw me from this point, sent me to Bath with a letter of recommendation introduc[ing] me to the celebrated Rauzzini who, tho' at a very advanced age, gave me lessons and, poor man, nearly expired in the very act of hearing me sing. While he lay there, almost senseless, and whose silence roused me from not hearing his *bravo*, I flew to his bedside, rang the bell, and soon learnt he had not strength enough to say farewell. A few hours [later] he was no more.[3] This was the master to the celebrated Billington, [Nancy] Storace, Incledon and Braham, the only surviving pupils with myself of this master.

On my return to London I sang, my father was pleased, and I made my first appearances for the benefit of Mr Braham and Mrs Billington, but found my voice yet not mature sufficiently for public exhibition,[4] and then withdrew till I appeared in a new opera at the English Opera House.

My success was all I could wish, and since which I have in this situation proposed to appear before you, my intention will be to present you with the necessary examples and requisites to study [to be] a vocalist. This may perhaps relieve you from the dull necessity of listening to song after song, and I trust, by a proper selection and variety, with an example of the nature, variety and the art of singing, an art that has eternal necessity, gives more pleasure, more passion, that excites mirth and implies awe to the religious, that gives ardour to the warriors, comfort to ....

If, in the course of this evening, I should diverge from the pedantic notes of a lecturer, it is only to relieve my hearers from that attendance which, from [i.e., upon] the most interesting subject, after

---

[3] Venanzio Rauzzini died in Bath on 8 April 1810.

[4] CEH had sung before then in private performances in London: for instance, the 1805 performances described above on pages 24 and 32–33.

a time becomes tedious, and the impression intended to [be] created is foiled by the matter of relief. Therefore, with every respect for my hearers, I plead for faults I may commit.

APPENDIX 3

CHARLES EDWARD HORN'S ACCOUNT OF
HIS FATHER IN A DRAFT LETTER TO
WILLIAM AYRTON
(1830)

Dear Sir,[1]

~~My affectionate and lamented father~~ Charles Frederick Horn was born at Nordhausen in Germany February 4th in the year 1762 and intended by his father to be a surveyor of lands. But a love for the science of music bore all a parent's authority before it. In vain were the instruments broken [and] sold, and as often purchased, and destroyed again by the intended surveyor's father, till the subject of this memoir determined to leave his native home and parents to visit the great cities of Europe.

After frugal and economical arrangements, during which time a celebrated counterpointist (Schroter),[2] who was an organist in

---

[1] This draft letter was the basis of the 'Biographical notice of the lately deceased Charles Frederick Horn' published in *The Harmonicon*, n.s. no. 34, October 1830, p 400–401. Although not named in the draft, the addressee presumably was *The Harmonicon*'s editor, William Ayrton, 1777–1858. CEH's draft includes many details omitted from the published account and clearly was written within a few weeks after CFH's burial on 7 August 1830. The *Harmonicon* notice was reprinted in New York in *The Albion*, 13 November 1830, p 181–182, without acknowledgement of its prior publication.

[2] Christoph Gottlieb Schröter, German organist, composer and theorist, 1699–1782, from 1732 to 1780 organist of St Nikolai, Nordhausen (see Johannes Schäfer, *Nordhäuser Orgelchronik*, Halle/Saale, 1939, p 80–81). Schröter and J. S. Bach were two of only 20 members of the Korrespondierenden Societät der Musikalische Wissenschaften which had been founded in 1738 by Lorenz Mizler von Kolof (German mathematician and writer on music, 1711–1778); presumably CFH's knowledge of and interest in Bach derived from Schröter's teaching. It may have been not just coincidence that CFH left Nordhausen about

Nordhausen, was the confidant and instructor of C. F. H. He set off for Paris with a determination to pursue his study and gain a livelihood by the profession he was bent upon pursuing, but chance gave him a companion, whose name were better left out, from his conduct, but who persuaded my father to go to London: that there was greater chance for a young practitioner. Which advice was followed, little thinking the intended motives of his seeming friend was to discharge his passage, and leave him [CFH] to shift as he could in a new country without friends [and] without money, for all had gone. However, arriving at the Thames, the friends parted upon no very good terms. And my father had left his box [of] clothes on board of the vessel, determining to see the great city and [to] return by the same conveyance to his native country.

I have often heard my father say He has often been heard to say that his fingers might speak a language his tongue could not. During this search [of London] on his landing, he met with a stranger and countryman who took him to Cheapside (Broderip's then, I believe, now Clementi's),[3] and told him 'if he could play as well as the pianists of that day' no doubt he would soon procure recommendations. His performance happened to [be] in the presence of His late Excellency the Saxon Ambassador Count Brühl in the year 1782, through whose kindness and confidence in my father, immediately took him to the late Marquis of Stafford, in whose house he became a resident and instructor to the three Ladies Leveson-Gower for several years (and where he met and married his present widow).[4]

Under their patronage he composed and dedicated his first work of *Six Sonatas for the Piano, Violin and Violoncello* to Lady Charlotte, the present Duchess of Beaufort. From this circumstance he was introduced by L[ady] Caroline Waldegrave[5] as instructor to

---

the time of Schröter's death there on 20 May 1782.

[3] See note 8 on page 2 above.

[4] 'Three' appears to be a mistake for 'two': see note 16 on page 4 above.

[5] Lady Caroline (see note 4 on page 73 above) subscribed to CFH's *Six Sonatas*. An undated letter from Susanna Leveson-Gower, Marchioness of Stafford, to her daughter Charlotte, now in the Special Collections Department of

Her late Majesty the Queen Charlotte and the Princesses Royal. Mr. Clementi had been appointed, but was under the necessity of visiting some of the foreign courts, and my father, Charles F. Horn, was left with his distinguished charge, which he retained till the year 1811 with honour and credit, that the affability and gracious condescension of the Royal Family was acknowledged to the last day of his existence.

He composed a second set of sonatas which were dedicated to Queen Charlotte, and a rondo in this set became the gauge and tension for years, during his many years' attendance on the Royal Family.[6]

He performed his duty faithfully and never solicited from them services or honours, which their kindness would never have refused, but he always induced them to suppose he had accumulated a large fortune. And I remember well when myself and brothers have urged him to request some advantage for us, which we thought from his continually being among them he was only to ask for and it would be granted, but he would reply 'If you knew how many favours were requested of that kind family daily, you would not urge one to make one more to trouble them'. Thus he never solicited but one favour, which was a letter for his son George, then in the East India Service.[7] He felt and appreciated the honourable situation he was holding ~~as the instructor of music to the Queen and Princesses~~, which often procured him the sanction and countenance of his last Majesty [i.e., King George IV] when Prince of Wales, also the Princes[ses].[8]

Birmingham University Information Services, ref. STA/2, indicates that Caroline Waldegrave and her maid had stayed with the Leveson-Gower family at Trentham Hall in the 1780s.

[6] CFH's *Three Sonatas for the Piano Forte or Harpsichord, with an Accompaniment for a Violin or Flute. Op. 2 Book 1*, was entered at Stationers' Hall on 15 March 1791.

[7] George John Horn became an officer cadet in the Indian Army in 1805 (British Library, Oriental and India Office, Cadet Papers, L/MIL/9/115/64–65) and a lieutenant in July 1807. He died on 18 July 1820 at Bangalore.

[8] However, none of CFH's compositions is preserved in the Royal Music Library formed by King George III and Queen Charlotte, which is now at the British Library. I am grateful to Dr Nicolas Bell of the British Library for this information.

He composed, about the year 1800, some military divertimentos by desire, and dedicated them to His Royal Highness the Duke of Cambridge,[9] also Twelve Themas with violin and violoncello accompaniment,[10] [and] a treatise on thorough bass.[11]

Also [he] was the first, in conjunction with S. Wesley,[12] to publish and introduce the celebrated fugues of Sebastian Bach in this country.[13] They were only known to a few professors previously to this. He also adapted them as quartettos which, in such fugues, where the four subjects are so correctly strictly kept in motion, certainly adds greatly to their effect, and [this] was a most ingenious mode of hearing them in perfection. In short, this style of music appears to have been his passion.

---

[9] Adolphus Frederick, 1774–1850, youngest son of King George III and Queen Charlotte, created Duke of Cambridge in 1801. CEH's statement appears to be mistaken. Although CFH dedicated his *A Sett of Twelve Fugues composed for the Organ by Sebastian Bach, arranged as Quartettos ...*, dated 15 January 1807, to the Duke of Cambridge, CFH's *A Collection of Divertimentos, for the Piano Forte*, which was entered at Stationers' Hall on 7 August 1804, is dedicated to HRH Princess Augusta.

[10] See note 7 on page 74 above.

[11] *A Treatise on Harmony with Practical Examples, and Thirty Studios, in all the Major and Minor Keys*. London, Royal Harmonic Institution. This book appears to have been published *c*1821 as it was printed from engraved plates bearing the number 893 (see O. W. Neighbour and Alan Tyson, *English Music Publishers' Plate Numbers in the First Half of the Nineteenth Century*, London, 1965, p 40).

[12] Samuel Wesley, composer and organist, 1766–1837.

[13] *S. Wesley and C. F. Horn's New and Correct Edition of the Preludes and Fugues, of John Sebastian Bach*. Book I of this edition was first published on 17 September 1810, Book II in early 1811, Book III in late 1811, and Book IV in 1813. See Kassler and Olleson, *Samuel Wesley (1766–1837): A Source Book*, *op. cit.*, p 690–691. Contrary to CEH's assertion, part 2 of the '48' had been published in London by Broderip and Wilkinson in 1808, and editions of the entire '48' had been imported into England from the continent before then. Detailed information about the circulation of the '48' in England before 1830 is given in Kassler (ed.), *The English Bach Awakening, op. cit.*

And, in the year 1823, he was appointed, through Dr Blomberg,[14] by his late Majesty George the Fourth, organist to his Majesty's Chapel Royal, Windsor,[15] which situation again brought him in continual presence of the king and his royal pupils Princess Augusta and [Princess Mary, now the] Duchess of Gloucester, by whom he was commanded to a musical evening and [to] perform the many lessons they had gone through 30 years ago. Their equal condescension and constancy after so long an absence appeared to have great effect on my father, as he would often say.

He was ill, nervous and not fit for the gay and *bon vivant* world, but he must be always ready when the king expected him.

During the few months' illness of his late lamented Majesty my father would often write music [and] amuse himself with writing down the marches and minuettos the king and Princess Augusta had composed, saying 'when the king gets well he will expect to find I have done something for him'. But when the news was brought to him not to be alarmed when the bell would toll, for the King was no more—this was 7 o'clock in the morning—, he shut up the book and said 'then my task is done and I shall write no more'.[16]

He gradually began to sink but tried in vain to rally. He could struggle to walk to see his friends, but when asked to write something in his books—his family knowing it was this terrific announcement—he did not refuse, but he never could be induced to so. On Tuesday the 3rd of August 1830, he talked cheerfully, made arrangements to visit his children in London on the following Thursday, called upon two or three friends near his residence in the Cloisters, returned home, passed the evening with his usual cheerfulness, spoke of his

---

[14] Rev. Frederick William Blomberg, 1761–1847, chaplain to the household of King George IV.

[15] However, according to the Chapter minutes of St George's Chapel, ref. VI.B.9, CFH was elected 'probationer' organist and 'master of the boys' on 30 June 1824, and on 30 September 1825 'Mr Horn having served his time as probationer organist and master of the boys was this day sworn and appointed organist and master of the boys in the room of Mr [William] Sexton [1764–1824] deceased'. I am grateful to Jude Dicken, Assistant Archivist of St George's Chapel, for this information.

[16] George IV died on 26 June 1830.

mother, whom he had after his father's death brought to England and buried,[17] and of his sisters whom, through a brother's affection[ate] care, have retired independent to their native country.[18] He retired to his bed at ½ 9 and, desiring the usual supper brought to him, he was found at 10 o'clock with his head sloped off his pillow as in a profound sleep, and without a groan expired at ½ past 10.

On the 3[d] he had appeared in much better spirits than usual, had walked to visit his children and friends, but after retiring to his bed he expired at ½ 10 without a groan, without a sigh.

He has left two sons, Charles Edward (the present composer and vocalist) [and] William,[19] and three daughters. His funeral was attended by his sons [and] 3 or private friends. The dean[20] and canons with the choir[21] performing the funeral anthem, and two of his boys, once his pupils, singing 'Hear my Prayer' as the tears trickled down the cheeks, the only reflection of the affection, regret and feeling his remains were accompanied with.[22]

He lies buried near the south door of the Chapel Royal, Windsor Castle, and a tablet to his memory bearing this inscription is placed in the Cloisters:

---

[17] See note 52 on page 20 above.

[18] It is not clear that more than one of CFH's two sisters came to England.

[19] William James Horn, music publisher and piano manufacturer. His addresses are listed (under both 'William Horn' and 'William James Horn') by John A. Parkinson, *Victorian Music Publishers: An Annotated List*, Warren, Michigan, 1990, p 134. William Horn published music by CFH, CEH and other composers, including (according to Parkinson) what may have been the first edition of *Pop Goes the Weasel*. George John Horn died in India in 1820. Frederick Thomas Horn's death date has not been found.

[20] Rev. Henry Lewis Hobart, 1774–1846, from 1816 dean of St George's Chapel, Windsor. I am grateful to Jude Dicken for providing his dates.

[21] Of St George's Chapel.

[22] On 2 November 1830, administration of CFH's estate, valued at £450, was granted to Diana Horn (Public Record Office, PROB 6/206 f 178[v]). She presumably continued to live in Windsor Castle after CFH's death, as she was buried at St George's Chapel on 20 August 1831 (Fellowes and Poyser, *The Baptism, Marriage and Burial Registers of St George's Chapel, Windsor, op. cit.*, p 254).

~~Sacred~~ to the Memory of Charles F. Horn
Organist to the Chapel Royal
Windsor
once Instructor of Music to the Royal Family
Died August 3 1830, aged 68
The Tablet is placed by his Eldest Son
Charles Edward[23]

As a theorist, excepting the celebrated Baumgarten with whom he was always upon the most intimate footing and friendship,[24] excepting when they differed upon his resolution of some abstruse discord which invariably tried their German obstinacy, at length chance would as often bring them together, upon a promise not to talk about music.[25]

Among his private pupils he had many amateurs who at that day were considered 'first rate', so that the celebrated Joseph Haydn once said to him, 'I have heard so many of your excellent pupils. I

---

[23] Permission to place this tablet in the Cloister was granted on 9 August 1830. Two letters by CEH summarised below—asking permission to erect the tablet and expressing thanks for this permission and for waiving of the £50 fee—are preserved in the archives of St George's Chapel. According to Edmund H. Fellowes, *Organists and Masters of the Choristers of St George's Chapel in Windsor Castle*, Windsor, 1939, p 70, this tablet is 'now removed to the West wall of the Dean's Cloister'. The inscription on the tablet reads: 'Sacred | to the memory of | Charles Frederick Horn | Organist of St George's Chapel, Windsor | Tutor in Music to her late Majesty | Queen Charlotte and the Princesses | He departed this life the 3rd of August, 1830 | Aged 68 | This tablet was placed here by | An affectionate son'.

[24] Charles Frederick Baumgarten, organist and musical theorist, *c*1738–1824.

[25] According to Purday, 'Memoir of C. E. Horn', *op. cit.*, p 558, CEH when a youth had received instruction from Baumgarten: 'Finding that Charles [CEH] required more attention to his studies than he [CFH] had time to bestow on them, his father engaged with the celebrated Baumgarten, the German musical theorist, to instruct him in the science of harmony and composition, remarking at the same time to Charles, "you are so rapid at invention that you will not give yourself time to think; a stranger may therefore have more control over you than I have, and I can explain to you any difficulties which may not be clear to your comprehension during your lessons."'

wish to dedicate some sonatas to one of them but do not know which'. And it was left to the master of the pupil [to decide]. Miss Wetenhall was the lady who won the prize and honour.[26]

Of his compositions, they are in the style of that day, and was thought to possess great brilliancy. And, no doubt, had not the accumulation of a family obliged him to make teaching his principal occupation, he would have written much more. Of public pupils who were under his tuition at different times as pianists were Braham, T[homas] Welsh, Mrs Billington, M. P. King for theory, and his son[27].

---

[26] See p 13 above.

[27] i.e., CEH himself.

APPENDIX 4

CHARLES EDWARD HORN'S DRAFT PETITION TO KING WILLIAM IV (*c*1830)

To His Most Gracious Majesty King William 4—in Council assembled

The humble petition of Charles Edward Horn eldest son of the late Charles Frederick Horn organist of your Most Gracious Majesty's Chapel Royal at Windsor deceased the 3rd August 1830[1]

Humbly sheweth

That your humble petitioner's father had the honour of being musical instructor to Your Majesty's mother the late Queen Charlotte and all the princesses of the royal family for 24 years.

That during that period your humble petitioner's father received an annual sum of £200 for the instruction of the royal family (excepting her late Majesty the Queen), for which a sum is now due amounting to £3000, & your humble petitioner's father being a German & not understanding the usages of this country, his warrant was not made out for life for the aforementioned sum of £200 *per ann*, as was the case with all the other instructors of the royal family, and consequently it was stopped by his late Majesty's ministers on or about the year 1814, although her late Majesty Queen Charlotte had given your humble petitioner's father her royal assurance it would be

---

[1] I thank Allison Derrett, Assistant Registrar of the Royal Archives, for the information that the papers of William IV were largely destroyed after his death in 1837, and that the Royal Archives now have no record that CEH's petition was received or was acted upon.

so, and a sum of — for the tuition of her Majesty which was not included in the afore[mentioned].

Your humble petitioner's father having died without having the least provision for his aged widow now 66 years of age, as well as a widowed daughter with two children,[2] the support of the former falls entirely on your humble petitioner.[3]

Your humble petitioner therefore supplicates your Most Gracious Majesty to take into your royal consideration his most unprecedented hard case, & to grant him for his life such annual allowances, as your Majesty shall deem just, which will enable him to support his aged mother.

For which

Your humble petitioner

as in duty bound

will forever pray

----

[2] CFH's daughter Sophia Horn, who married Daniel Sewell at St Pancras Old Church on 20 December 1821 (IGI). In the 1851 census, Sophia Sewell, 'professor of music', is recorded as a widow and as head of the household in which her unmarried sister Louisa Horn, a 'retired housekeeper', and her unmarried son George Sewell, a 'stationer', also lived. I am grateful to Colin Gowing for obtaining the census record.

[3] In 1850, an advertisement on the front page of *The Critic of Books, Engravings, Music, and Decorative Art*, v 9 no. 212 (1 February 1850), asserted that 'Miss Horn [i.e., Louisa] was wholly dependant [sic] upon her brother [CEH]'.

APPENDIX 5

THE HORN FAMILY

The three trees that follow provide genealogical information about the immediate families of Charles Frederick Horn, his wife Diana Arboneau Dupont, and their son Charles Edward Horn. The marriage of Charles Edward Horn's son, Charles, to Jeannette Prosser in 1833 did not last; he remarried in 1854. He had several children, of whom numerous descendants are alive today.

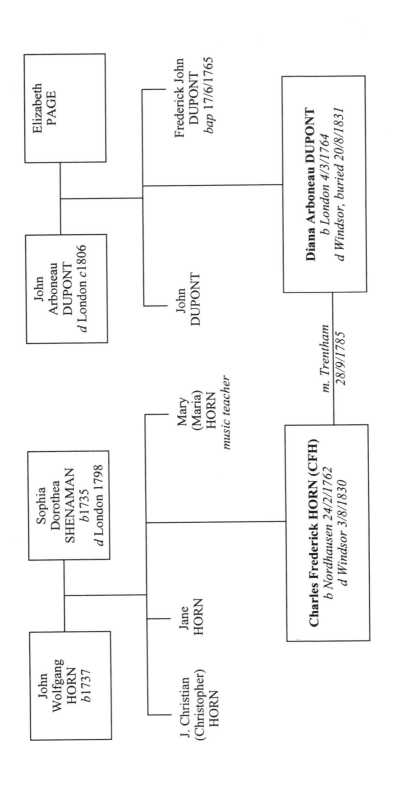

Charles Frederick Horn, Diana Arboneau Dupont and their Families

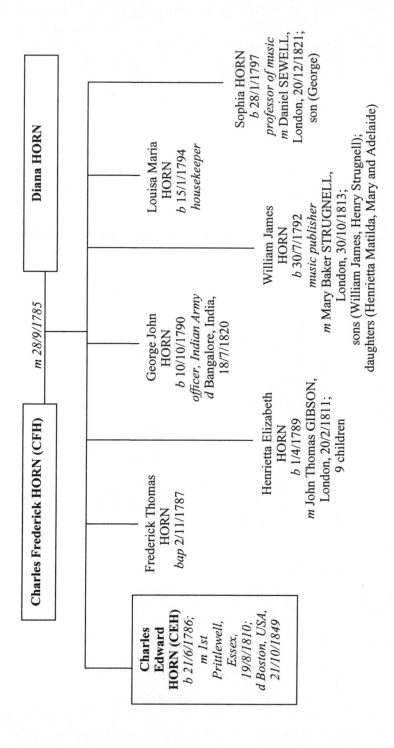

The Children of Charles Frederick and Diana Horn, all baptised in London

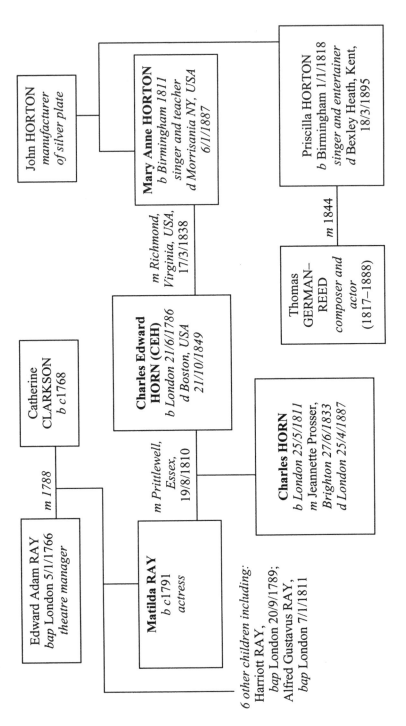

Charles Edward Horn's Wives and their Families

APPENDIX 6

CORRESPONDENCE OF
THE HORN FAMILY

The following correspondence of Charles Frederick Horn, Charles Edward Horn, Matilda Horn and Mary Anne Horn has come to my attention. An exhaustive search for extant letters has not been made and the list below almost certainly is incomplete.

CHARLES FREDERICK HORN (1762–1830)

location of manuscript unknown; letter printed in CFH's song *Trafalgar* published in London by Goulding, Phipps, d'Almaine & Co.

- 24/12/1805 letter to Abraham Goldsmid, to whom CFH dedicates his song *Trafalgar* as thanks for the 'many acts of friendship' that Goldsmid has conferred upon him 'for a series of years'.

Royal College of Music, London, Ms 2130 letter 17

- 1/10/1809? letter from Samuel Wesley, discussing the sale of the edition of J. S. Bach's organ sonatas [BWV 525–530] prepared jointly by CFH and Wesley, and noting public demand for their forthcoming edition of Bach's '48'.[1]

Glasgow University Library, Euing Collection, R.d. 86/105

- 31/10/1823 autobiographical letter to the compiler of the *Biographical Dictionary of Musicians* [printed in Appendix 1 above].[2]

---

[1] This letter has no salutation or date and its address portion has not been preserved. For the identification of CFH as recipient and the assigned date of this letter, see Kassler and Olleson, *Samuel Wesley (1766–1837): A Source Book, op. cit.*, p 268. The full text of this letter is printed in Philip Olleson (ed.), *The Letters of Samuel Wesley: Professional and Social Correspondence, 1797–1837*, Oxford, 2001, p 125–126.

[2] The beginning of this letter is reproduced facing page 22.

British Library, London,   • 13/1/1830 letter to Vincent Novello (1781–
Add Ms 11730 f 75–76   1861), enclosing music and regretting that ill
         health prevents CFH from attending Novello's
         'musical party'. CFH now believes that he was
         mistaken in claiming that the first fugue in his set
         of 12 fugues[3] was by J. S. Bach. He thinks that
         this fugue was composed by Bach's son, Carl
         Philipp Emanuel Bach.

Guildhall Library,   • 16/3/1830 letter to William Hawes concerning
London, Ms 10189/1 f 72   CFH's 'old friend and scholar', Thomas Foster
         Barham (1766–1844) of Leskinnick, Cornwall,
         who had asked CFH to get singers.

CHARLES EDWARD HORN (1786–1849)

Yomiuri Shimbun   *About 62 drafts or copies of letters by CEH:*
Symphony Orchestra,   • 9/9/1828 letter from New York to Mr Cowell
Tokyo, in the same   in Boston, concerning terms for performances by
volume as CEH's   CEH and others there.
Memoirs   • A series of 1829 letters to Charles Kemble
         (then manager of Covent Garden Theatre), Sir
         George Smart and others, regarding CEH's
         meeting with Kemble at Liverpool, CEH's
         agreement to perform at Covent Garden for £10
         per week for a short time until the theatre can
         afford to pay him £16 per week, CEH's refusal to
         play a part he considered unsuitable, his being
         'forfeited' £3/3/- for missing a rehearsal because
         he had been invited to perform at Frogmore (a
         royal residence in Windsor), his resignation from
         Covent Garden after three weeks, his agreement to
         repay the £28 he had received from the theatre,
         and the hardship that this has caused.

---

[3] *A Sett of Twelve Fugues, Composed for the Organ by Sebastian Bach, Arranged as Quartettos ... by C. F. Horn.* London, 1807.

Yomiuri Shimbun Symphony Orchestra *(continued)*	• 1830 letter to 'Sir' seeking employment for his son Charles who is 'of good principles, speaks French, writes a fine hand and is an excellent accountant', and saying that a 'misunderstanding' has released CEH from Covent Garden and he 'should now be delighted to return to Drury Lane'. • 1830 letter to William Ayrton [printed in Appendix 3 above], containing an obituary of CFH. • 1831 letters to Thomas Welsh and to Mr Stapleton (treasurer of the Theatre Royal, Dublin), seeking particulars of the £128 'paid into Rowland Stephenson's bank' that CEH had received in 1822 for his services in Dublin.[4]
Royal College of Music, London Ms 6879B	*3 letters by CEH:* • 30/8/1817 letter to Robert William Elliston at Birmingham, remarking that Elliston did not keep his appointment with CEH at Stratford Place [Elliston's London home], and noting that Matilda Horn has given CEH Elliston's letter offering her two months work at Birmingham and Leicester, which she would accept if Elliston could agree to the more favourable terms that CEH proposes.
Ms 6876E	• 26/5/1826 letter to William a'Beckett (solicitor, 1777–1855?), at whose advice CEH has signed a draft, and upon whom CEH is relying to be kept 'out of any expense or trouble'.
Ms 2193	• 29/10/1845 letter to Edward Taylor (1784–1863, professor of music at Gresham College) forwarding a glee for the college and giving Taylor CEH's cantata. CEH is about to go to Leeds for four nights to lecture.

---

[4] This bank, of which CEH's godfather Edward Stephenson was a partner, failed after Stephenson's son-in-law Rowland Stephenson (1782–1856) fled to America in 1829. Thomas Welsh and the Royal Harmonic Institution (of which Welsh was a director) were much involved with this bank, and in 1831 its administrators were still endeavouring to account for transactions made in prior years.

New-York Historical
Society, New York

- 16/9/1817 letter to R. W. Elliston at Birmingham, regarding CEH's plans to be with him at Leicester on 6/10/1817 and at Birmingham on 13/10/1817, and listing proposed performances that include appearances by CEH's pupil Miriam H. Buggins [*later* Miriam Hammersley].

University of Missouri—
Kansas City Libraries,
Special Collections
Department

11 letters by CEH:

- 9/7/1819 written from Dublin to George Robins, promoting Miriam Hammersley as a singer and actress suitable for Drury Lane Theatre, and asking Robins to reply to CEH at Cork.
- 9/7/1819 to Elliston, noting Elliston's launch 'into poor Drury' [Lane] and hoping that 'all our past grievances' can be forgotten, as CEH would like to take the lead in an opera there and would like Elliston to engage Miriam Hammersley.
- 11/9/1819 to Elliston from Limerick, negotiating fees for CEH and Miriam Hammersley.
- 16/5/1820 to Elliston from Cheltenham, regarding Elliston's high price for the Northampton Theatre and CEH's interest to rent the Olympic Theatre next season.
- 4/6/1824 to 'Dear Sir' about arrangements for singing 'God save the King' this evening.
- undated *c*1824 letter to Henry Hill (1781–1839) of the firm Monzani and Hill, asking at what hour Mme Giuditta Pasta (1797–1865) will sing.
- 26/5/1825 to James Winston seeking payment.
- 6/5/1826 to Elliston protesting about being cast in a part that CEH gave up two years ago.
- 22/5/1833 from New York to Col. George Pope Morris (author and publisher, 1802–1864), concerning a rondo that CEH has dedicated to him.
- undated letter to Nicholas Mori (violinist and music publisher, *c*1796–1839), regarding payment for CEH's 'six songs'.
- undated letter to 'Dear Sir' requesting free admissions [to a performance].

British Library,
London

Add Ms 33965 f 56–57

Add Ms 52337A f 186

2 letters by CEH with 1 draft letter to CEH:

- 19/6/1821 from CEH to the music seller and publisher Thomas Williams, with Williams's draft reply. CEH's forthcoming benefit 'is to be the wind up of all my troubles'. He wishes the Misses Ashe (daughters of Andrew Ashe, flautist, *c*1759–1838) to sing either his trio 'Hark! Italy's Music' or his trio 'No mother no', and desires Williams's opinion. Williams asks CEH to return manuscripts and will then reply to his question.
- 29/4/1843 to William Ayrton, saying that CEH has taken the Store Street rooms in London to try his cantata [*The Christmas Bells*, on 18/5/1843]; he hopes that Ayrton and his daughter can attend.

Harvard University,
Houghton Library,
Harvard Theatre
Collection

All letters shelved as
uncatalogued ALS except
for the following letters,
which have been assigned
specific call numbers:

13/8/1820
 TS 1001.5, p 110

14/2/1821 and 17/7/1821
 TS 937.4, v 21, facing
 p 292

31/5/1824
 Opera collection, p 27

10/7/1824
 TS 953.6F, v 1 part II,
 opposite p 134

7/2/1825
 TS 931.2, v 3 no. 6 part
 I, facing p 137

21 letters by CEH:

- 13/8/1820 from Newcastle upon Tyne to Elliston, regarding CEH's proposal for next season and requesting a reply at the Edinburgh theatre.
- 14/2/1821 to Joseph Shepherd Munden at Drury Lane Theatre, at whose request CEH has left some music that he hopes will be satisfactory.
- letter docketed 17/7/1821 to Mr Millington 'about payments for Society Arts dinner'; CEH, who is leaving town, asks if he can refer to Millington 'the gentlemen who I engaged to your dinner'.
- 31/5/1824 to Elliston, saying that he cannot remain with Elliston unless he gets £2 per week more than his current salary, for three years.
- 10/7/1824 from Glasgow to Elliston at Drury Lane. CEH acknowledges receipt of a copy of Matilda Horn's correct response to Elliston's letter [her 4/7/1824 letter to Elliston entered below]. CEH was pained to leave but, while away from London, his income is £50 to £60 a week, much more than his 'moderate' Drury Lane salary. CEH can return in early August if Elliston wants, and apologises for any misunderstanding. Elliston can reply to CEH at Edinburgh.
- 7/2/1825 to 'Dear Sir', declining 20 guineas, which is 10 guineas lower than that offered to CEH by [Nicholas] Bochsa (composer and harpist, 1789–1856). CEH would accept 30 guineas.

Harvard Theatre
Collection *(continued)*

6/9/1825
   TS 952.2F, v 3 p 109

23/11/1827
   TS 939.5.3F, v 1 part II,
   no. 71

1/1/1844
   TS 990.1, v 2 p 44

•   6/9/1825 letter from Dublin to James Winston, saying that CEH has done better than expected in Dublin, performing Caspar [in *Der Freischütz*], and will earn £300 if he returns to Dublin in November, for which CEH asks Winston to obtain Elliston's approval.

•   undated *c*1825 letter to Winston, returning 'the part of Sir John Loverule' [in the ballad opera *The Devil to Pay* by Charles Coffey, Irish playwright, *d*1745] which CEH declines, as Elliston had promised that CEH 'should not play parts that were allotted to another department' and he finds the part 'very disagreeable'. CEH will be happy to assist concerning 'Mrs Carr's business'.[5]

•   undated *c*1825 letter to Winston, saying that CEH will not sing the song he previously sang in *Love in a Village* at Drury Lane, but will sing instead a new song he has published called 'Slighted Love'. Winston should insert this information in the bills.[6]

•   2/6/1827 letter to 'My dear Sir', thanking the addressee for his kind attention during CEH's 'short stay' in Covent Garden and apologising for any unintended slight in not supplying him with a book; this mistake will be rectified next week.

•   23/11/1827 from Baltimore to Francis Courtney Wemyss (actor and theatre manager, 1797–1859) in Philadelphia, with Wemyss's 26/11/1827 reply, regarding a dispute relating to CEH's performances in Philadelphia.[7]

•   30/11/1827 from Baltimore, regretting that CEH cannot accept the invitation from the St Andrew's Society in that city.

---

[5] Perhaps a reference to the actress 'Miss Carr' who performed with CEH at Drury Lane Theatre in December 1824. See Nelson and Cross (eds.), *Drury Lane Journal, op. cit.*, p 103.

[6] The publication 'Slighted Love, a favorite rondo, introduced ... in the opera of *Love in a Village* ... by Charles E. Horn' is dated *c*1825 by the British Library. Winston resigned from Drury Lane Theatre on 30 June 1827 (Nelson and Cross, *op. cit.*, p 160 note 6); therefore, this letter was written before then.

[7] In 1828, Wemyss was fined $1,000 for assaulting CEH. See Montague, *Charles Edward Horn, op. cit.*, p 28.

Harvard Theatre
Collection *(continued)*

- 11/11/1829 to James William Wallack at Drury Lane, hoping that Wallack can spare an hour 'to hear the alteration made in *The Magic Flute*', which CEH thinks will bring 'a great deal of money' to the Theatre. CEH remarks that, although this opera is considered Mozart's masterpiece, 'the plot was so infernal'.
- 24/5/1831 to John Pritt Harley (actor and singer, 1786–1858), naming the songs that CEH wishes to sing and regretting that his name was not put in Harley's bills announcing the show.
- 15/7/1835 from New York to William Trotter Porter (journalist, 1809–1858), marked 'private', asking Porter, in anything he may write, 'not to allude to my son's late profession'.[8] CEH's son's musical training 'has been done in a very short time', entirely by CEH. His son sings in 'the pure English style with little ornament' but with 'studied expression'.
- 5/11/1838 from Boston to Francis Courtney Wemyss at the Walnut Street Theatre, Philadelphia, saying that, from the treatment CEH and his wife[Mary Anne] received at the Chestnut Street Theatre, Philadelphia, he has determined that she will never appear on the stage again.
- 7/2/1839 from New York to Henry Russell (presumably the composer, 1812–1900), regretting that CEH may have mistakenly uttered opinions 'injurious' to Russell, and hoping that they can remain on good terms.
- undated, docketed 10/1843, letter to William Thomas Moncrieff (actor, 1794–1857), saying that CEH has shown Moncrieff's 'piece' to [James] Wallack, and asking Moncrieff's opinion of *The Muleteer*.

---

[8] At this time Porter edited the weekly New York journal *Spirit of the Times*. Charles Horn's 'late profession' may have been accountancy; see the 1830 letter from CEH to 'Sir' entered on page 97 above.

Harvard Theatre
Collection *(continued)*

- . 1/1/1844 to Thomas Mackinlay [of the music publishing firm D'Almaine & Co.] regarding CEH's sacred cantata *The Christmas Bells* [published by that firm], which is now 'your property', and conveying CEH's disappointment not to have received copies of this work 'which have been so repeatedly promised'.
- 22/1/1847 to Benjamin Nottingham Webster (actor and theatre manager, 1797–1882), asking him to search through bills of the Haymarket Theatre [which Webster then managed] to find 'when *Paul Pry* came out' [an opera that included CEH's much performed song 'Cherry Ripe'], as CEH's 'interests are very much concerned with that event'.[9]
- 29/7/1847 to Joseph Alfred Novello (music publisher, 1810–1896). CEH has composed, and wishes to sell, four trios that can be performed by two sopranos and a contralto or by a choir. CEH would take half of the payment [for the copyright of these trios] in Novello publications.

Historical Society of
Pennsylvania,
Philadelphia, located as
indicated:

Dreer collection,
  Musicians

5 letters by CEH:

- 19/8/1820 from Newcastle-upon-Tyne to Samuel Thomas Russell (*c*1770–1845, then stage manager, Drury Lane Theatre), concerning correspondence with Elliston regarding CEH's return to Drury Lane, and seeking Russell's help in the negotiations. Provided that CEH is given 'an equal chance' for public favour he would not object to performing in the same operas as [John] Braham.

Gratz collection,
  ABC series

- 28/5/1833 to Mr Duffy[10] at Albany, New York, saying that CEH and Miss [Elizabeth] Hughes (a singer who was a pupil of CEH) will be happy to play there on their way to Canada.[11]

---

[9] *Paul Pry* received its first performance at the Haymarket Theatre on 13 September 1825.

[10] CEH's spelling of this name is not clear.

[11] Montague, *Charles Edward Horn, op. cit.*, p 36–37, describes Elizabeth Hughes as CEH's 'most famous pupil'.

Historical Society of Pennsylvania *(continued)*	• 4/6/1838 to Gen. George Pope Morris, saying that Mrs [Mary Anne] H[orn] has sung Morris's song and asking whether he has pieces that would
Gratz collection, case 13 box B	suit her. CEH's sister, son and son's wife are with him. CEH plans to remain 'in town for good', to instruct, conduct and sing; however, he has 'done with the stage'.
Gratz collection, ABC series	• 26/7/1843 to Robert Shelton Mackenzie (author and journalist, 1809–1881), thanking him for noticing CEH's composition *Christmas Bells* in the *Court Magazine*.
Society collection	• 4/8/1846 to Gen. Morris, introducing and recommending John Macfarren (artist, 1818–1901).
New York Public Library, Music Division, *MNY	*4 letters by CEH relating to Drury Lane Theatre:* • 7/10/1822 to 'Dear Sir' [presumably Elliston, see CEH's 20/10/1822 letter at Indiana University entered below], stating that the addressee's proposal of £10 a week for three years is 'too little' for CEH to accept; he proposes instead £12, £13 and £14 a week for these years. CEH 'was misled the season before last' by the addressee preventing his 'writing for any other house or accepting…a large school offered to me'. If CEH's proposal is accepted he will devote himself exclusively to Drury Lane. • 4/11/1824 to James Winston, saying that although Mr Elliston gave him four [theatre admissions] he is one short, as 'some Indian relations are with us'. • undated letter to James Winston, requesting that the line 'first appearance in that character' be 'put in' [an announcement of a performance], as CEH likes 'to make a splash'. • undated *c*1825 letter to James Winston, proposing performances of *The Beggar's Opera* and *The Barber of Seville* and suggesting casts that include Catherine Stephens and Madame Vestris.[12]

---

[12] 1825 seems the likely year because the letter refers both to *Abon Hassan*, which opened at Drury Lane on 4/4/1825 with CEH performing the title role, and to 'Harley's night', presumably the 31/5/1825 benefit at Drury Lane for John Pritt Harley which was advertised in *John Bull*, 29/5/1825, p 169.

Indiana University, Lilly Library, S. C. Woodward manuscripts	• 20/10/1822 letter to George Robins. CEH has received through Thomas John Dibdin,[13] but cannot accept, Elliston's offer of £10 per week for one year. CEH wants £12 per week and 'will not enter any theatre anymore without three years certain engagement'. Earlier, Elliston had told CEH 'publicly' in the green room that 'we should never part on any terms', and had agreed to pay CEH £16 per week for three years.
Pierpont Morgan Library, New York, Mary Flagler Cary Music Collection	*2 letters by CEH to unknown recipients:* • 28/6/1823 letter regarding correspondence with Elliston about hiring CEH and 'Mrs H' [Matilda Horn]. • 21/12/1824 letter stating that Elliston agreed to admit Matilda's brother 'Mr Ray' and two friends for free.
Collection of Jamie and Michael Kassler, Northbridge NSW, Australia	• 10/12/18[24?][14] letter to Messrs Sainsbury and Co. Because CEH has 'the most urgent use for every shilling for two or three months', he regretfully is returning 'the books' left with him [presumably the two volumes of Sainsbury and Co.'s *Biographical Dictionary of Musicians*] until he finds it 'convenient' to pay for them.
Oberlin College Library, Oberlin, Ohio, Special Collections, Thomas Goodwin Collection, AM401.G66, Series I, in Box 1	*3 letters by CEH:* • Undated 1828 letter from Philadelphia, asking Thomas Goodwin (music copyist and librarian, 1799–1886) to send from New York CEH's full score of [Thomas Arne's opera] *Artaxerxes* [which opened, with CEH in the part of Artabenes, at the Chestnut Street Theatre, Philadelphia, on 7/5/1828].[15]

---

[13] Dibdin had just become stage manager of Drury Lane Theatre. See Nelson and Cross, *Drury Lane Journal, op. cit.*, p 57.

[14] The last two digits of the year have been destroyed by a tear in the page. 1824 is suggested as the likely year because Sainsbury and Co.'s *Biographical Dictionary of Musicians*, which contained articles about both CFH and CEH, was published in October 1824. The beginning of this letter is reproduced facing page 55.

[15] Montague, *Charles Edward Horn, op. cit.*, p 28.

Oberlin College Library *(continued)*

- 'Wednesday morn' 1829 letter to Thomas Goodwin, presenting the programme for the forthcoming 'New York Grand Musical Festival' at Niblo's 'new and splendid saloon' on Broadway, and seeking Goodwin's help with preparations for this concert [which took place, under CEH's general direction, on 18/5/1829].[16]
- 'Sunday morning' letter to 'My dear Sir', acknowledging that Mr [Edmund Shaw] Simpson (manager of the Park Theatre, New York) has allowed the recipient to perform two parts in *Macbeth*, but strongly recommending that the recipient not do this, as CEH wants the performance standard in New York 'to come as near Drury Lane and Covent Garden as we can'.

St George's Chapel Archives, Windsor Castle, Berkshire, I.A.4

2 letters by CEH written from Windsor Castle:
- 6/8/1830 to the Dean [Rev. Henry Lewis Hobart, 1774–1846] and Chapter of St George's Chapel, requesting permission to erect a tablet in memory of CFH in the Cloisters near St George's Chapel.
- 15/8/1830 to William de St Croix (1787–1843, from 1827 chapter clerk to the royal college of St George, Windsor), thanking him for his 8/8/1830 letter [not preserved] granting permission to place a memorial to CFH in the Cloisters. The Dean told CEH yesterday that the £50 fee would be dispensed with, in consideration of the 'high esteem' in which CFH was held. CEH asks how long his mother 'may occupy the organist's house', so that he 'may make preparations for her removal'.

---

[16] See Mason, *Sketches and Impressions ... from the After-Dinner Talk of Thomas Goodwin, op. cit.*, p 280–282.

Library of Congress, Washington, Music Division, ML95.H45 Case, Box 3, p 817–818

• 30/1/1843 to Anthony Philip Heinrich (composer, 1781–1861), regarding payment for the engraved plates from which three compositions by Heinrich were printed in New York. CEH promises to call upon a mutual friend when he gets to London.[17]

University of Texas, Austin, Harry Ransom Humanities Research Center, Theater Collection

4 undated letters by CEH:
• 2 notes to Henry Phillips (baritone, 1801–1876), one written about April 1843 asking Phillips to sing in CEH's cantata at CEH's benefit concert planned for Tuesday 9 May [1843].
• 2 letters to Alfred Bunn (author and theatre manager, 1796–1860), one mentioning that CEH has heard *The Bohemian Girl* [an opera for which Bunn wrote the libretto],[18] the other regretting that CEH cannot sing tomorrow night.

Mitchell Library, Sydney, Australia Ms A 12 letter 33

• 'Wednesday night', about June–August 1843, letter to Thomas Mackinlay, offering to sell [to Mackinlay's firm, D'Almaine & Co.] the copyright of CEH's cantata [*The Christmas Bells*] for a payment of 100 guineas or for an alternative financial arrangement that CEH proposes.[19]

Folger Shakespeare Library, Washington, Ms Add 1052

• 24/1/1844 letter to J. Webster, complaining that, at Webster's theatre last night, CEH heard his music for *The Merry Wives of Windsor* played without him receiving credit as its composer.

---

[17] The text of this letter is printed in William Treat Upton, *Anthony Philip Heinrich: A nineteenth-century Composer in America*, New York, 1939, p 177.

[18] Hence this letter was written after that opera's first performance at Drury Lane on 27 November 1843.

[19] This letter can be dated after 18/5/1843 because CEH apparently enclosed with it the accompanying bill (at the Mitchell Library) for the 18/5/1843 performance of his cantata *The Christmas Bells* at the Store Street Rooms in London. This letter presumably was written before September 1843, as CEH wanted the cantata published by November. CEH's letter to Thomas Mackinlay of 1/1/1844 (at Harvard Theatre Collection, noted above) states that Mackinlay now owned this cantata.

Special Collections, Tutt Library, Colorado College, Colorado Springs, Colorado, Ms 0145 (Alice Bemis Taylor Collection), in v 1	• undated, *c*1844 letter to Charles Mackay (author, 1814–1819), stating that CEH has again taken up *The Salamandrine* [a book by Mackay, published in 1842]. CEH has 'succeeded much better' than he had when he showed Mackay his work 'in the winter', and thanks Mackay for his 'grand' notice of CEH in *The [Morning] Chronicle* [of which Mackay was assistant subeditor from 1834 to 1844].[20]
Garrick Club, London	• Undated 'Thursday night' letter to 'Gentlemen', saying that CEH had considered Mrs [Matilda] Horn's 'engagement as fixed for the present season' but has found that she 'was not engaged'. CEH has consulted his friend Mr [Alexander] Rae (actor, 1782–1820, from 1817 Drury Lane stage manager), 'through whose interest' she was 're-established'. CEH asks whether Matilda can be engaged for two or three years, as this would 'very materially direct' his 'own pursuits'.
Huntington Library, San Marino, California, Planché papers	• Undated note to James Robinson Planché (dramatist, 1796–1880).
Southern Illinois University at Edwardsville, Tollefson collection	• Letter dated 'Wednesday morning' to Robert Shelton Mackenzie, concerning Mackenzie's copy of a book by Gen. George Pope Morris.
location of manuscript unknown; not seen; letter offered for sale as item 218 in catalogue no. 33 of Messrs Ellis, London, 1933	• 2/7/1822 letter from 5 Westmorland Street [Dublin] to Elliston at Drury Lane Theatre. According to the catalogue description this letter refers to Charles Lamb, Mary Anne Wilson and her future husband Thomas Welsh.

---

[20] Letter presumably written after CEH's 15/3/1843 return to London from America and, from the referene to a past winter, presumably not before 1844. Letter presumably not written after 1844, when Mackay moved to Glasgow to become editor of *The Glasgow Argus*.

location of manuscript unknown; letter printed on p 2 of publication of CEH's canzonette by Collard & Collard in London[21]

• 6/7/1833 letter from New York to Henry Rowley Bishop, whose talent CEH has 'always' admired, hoping that CEH's canzonette 'His words upon the paper burn', dedicated to Bishop, will be worthy of his notice, even though CEH and Bishop are now 3,000 miles apart.

MATILDA HORN (*b c*1791)

Folger Shakespeare Library, Washington, Ms Add 1051

• 14/8/1819 letter to James Winston, stating that she has written to R. W. Elliston regarding the possibility of her being engaged by Drury Lane Theatre and adding that CEH is 'too far off' to aid her solicitation. A pencilled note on the letter says that it was answered 'no' on 17/8/1819.

Harvard University, Houghton Library, Harvard Theatre Collection, uncatalogued ALS

• 4/7/1824 letter to Elliston, saying that CEH left London yesterday believing that James Winston had told Elliston of this. CEH had made engagements in Scotland before he knew that Elliston had determined to keep Drury Lane Theatre open all summer, and had 'concluded his treaty with the Glasgow and Edinburgh managers' during the interval of Elliston's 'indecision' whether to accept CEH's terms for the next three years.

---

[21] A copy of this publication is at the British Library, shelf-mark H.1300(17).

MARY ANNE HORN (1811–1887)

Harvard University,
Houghton Library,
Harvard Theatre
Collection:

uncatalogued ALS

2 letters by Mary Anne Horn:

• 25/9/1838 letter from New York to Lewis J.
Cist (poet, composer and autograph collector,
1818–1885) at Cincinnati, Ohio, saying that CEH
has copied one of his favourite songs 'composed
shortly after the death of his mother' for the
recipient's valuable autograph collection.[22]
Although CEH and Mary Anne were cordially
received at Cincinnati they are now 'settled down
quietly in private life', so there is 'no chance' of
their returning to Cincinnati soon.

TS 939.5.3, v 2 part IV,
no. 103

• 2/8/1874 letter signed 'M. A. Züst' from West
Hoboken, New Jersey, to Charles Mason,
requesting him to give her 'quarterly stipends' to
Mr Horton, her brother.

---

[22] This manuscript, dated 1838, of CEH's song 'Mother, Oh sing me to rest' (the
words written by Felicia Hemans, poet, 1793–1835), appeared as lot 2415 in the
*Catalogue of the Valuable Collection of Autographs ... the Property of Lewis J.
Cist, Esq., lately deceased ... to be sold at auction ... October 5th, 6th, 7th and
8th, 1886 ... [by] Bangs & Co., New York City* (New York, 1886). It was sold
for $1.75, according to a priced copy of this catalogue in the library of Jamie
and Michael Kassler, Northbridge NSW, Australia. I am grateful to Annette
Fern of the Harvard Theatre Collection for locating uncatalogued Horn family
documents there, including the manuscript of this song.

APPENDIX 7

CHRONOLOGY

The following chronology lists selected datable events in the lives of Charles Frederick Horn and Charles Edward Horn. With few exceptions, events after the period covered by CEH's memoirs have been excluded. Unless noted below, the source of each of the statements below is given in the preceding texts or in the footnotes that accompany them. The date of entry of a work at Stationers' Hall can be presumed to be its date of publication.[1]

24/2/1762	CFH born at Nordhausen, Germany.
20/5/1782	CFH's teacher, the organist Christoph Gottlieb Schröter, dies at Nordhausen.
1782	CFH arrives in London with little money and almost immediately is found a position as music master to Georgiana Augusta Leveson-Gower and Charlotte Sophia Leveson-Gower at Trentham Hall, Staffordshire.
28/9/1785	At Trentham, CFH marries Diana Dupont, a governess and French teacher of the Leveson-Gower children.
1786; <5/1786	CFH and Diana move to 12 St Martins Street, Leicester Fields, London.
29/5/1786	CFH's *Six Sonatas for the Piano Forte*, op. 1, dedicated to Charlotte Sophia Leveson-Gower, entered at Stationers' Hall.
21/6/1786	CEH born at 12 St Martins Street.

---

[1] See Michael Kassler (ed.), *Music Entries at Stationers' Hall, 1710–1818*, Aldershot, 2004, forthcoming.

15/7/1786	CEH baptised at St Martin-in-the-Fields, Westminster; his godfathers are Edward Stephenson and John Peter Salomon.
16/11/1786	CFH's adaptation for the pianoforte of *A Favorite Overture by Giuseppe Haydn* (from Haydn's symphony no. 76) entered at Stationers' Hall.
2/11/1787	Frederick Thomas Horn, brother of CEH, baptised at St Mary's Marylebone Road, indicating that CFH and his family had moved to this parish before then.
1788	CFH subscribes for 10 copies of part 3 of Johann Wilhelm Hässler's *Sechs leichte Sonaten*.[2]
1/4/1789	Henrietta Elizabeth Horn, sister of CEH, baptised at St Mary's Marylebone Road (IGI).
1789; >5/1789	CFH and family remove to a rented house in Dean's Yard, Windsor; their neighbours are the Papendiek family. CFH's mother Sophia Dorothea Horn and his sister (probably Mary Horn) have come from Germany and are living with CFH.
29/6/1789	CFH becomes music master to Their Royal Highnesses the princesses at an annual salary of £200.
20/10/1789	CFH commanded to attend Queen Charlotte twice weekly as her music master, apparently without fee.
10/10/1790	George John Horn, brother of CEH, born. He was baptised on 8/11/1790 at St Mary's, Marylebone Road.
<3/1791	CFH and family return to London and live at 73 Upper Norton Street, Portland Road, although he and they go back and forth to Windsor.
4/2/1791	*Three Sonatas for the Piano-forte* by Cecilia Maria Barthelemon, to which CFH subscribed, entered at Stationers' Hall.
15/3/1791	CFH's *Three Sonatas for the Piano Forte*, op. 2, dedicated to Queen Charlotte, entered at Stationers' Hall.

---

[2] CFH also subscribed for one copy of part 4 of this work, published in 1790. Hässler (German composer, 1747–1822) was in London from 1790 to 1792.

*c*1792	CFH and his family remove to 4 Pratt Street, Lambeth, a house rented from the stockbroker Edward Wetenhall. CFH instructs Wetenhall's daughter, Ann Wetenhall, and considers her his finest pianoforte pupil.
6/3/1792	CFH's arrangement of movements from Mozart's serenade K. 320, published by Longman and Broderip, entered at Stationers' Hall.
30/7/1792	William James Horn, brother of CEH, born. He was baptised on 25/9/1792 at St James, Piccadilly.
1793	To curtail expenses, CFH and his family remove to a smaller house in Charles Street, China Row, Lambeth.
9/3/1793	John Bland's publication of Leopold Koželuch's *Three Sonatas for the Piano Forte*, op. 38, entered at Stationers' Hall. This publication is dedicated to 'Miss Wetenhall', apparently at CFH's recommendation.
9/10/1793	CFH's engagement as Queen Charlotte's music master ends. He continues as music master to Their Royal Highnesses the princesses.
15/1/1794	Louisa Maria Horn, sister of CEH, born. She was baptised on 23/4/1794 at St Mary's, Lambeth.
5/2/1794	CFH's *Three Sonatas for the grand & small Piano Forte*, published by Longman & Broderip, entered at Stationers' Hall.
11/1/1796	CFH's *Twelve Country Dances for the Year 1796* entered at Stationers' Hall.
28/1/1797	Sophia Horn, sister of CEH, born. She was baptised on 1/1/1798 at St Mary's, Lambeth.
30/3/1798	CFH's mother Sophia Horn buried at St Mary's, Lambeth.
*c*9/1799	CFH and 'Miss Horn' (presumably CFH's sister Mary) subscribe to Haydn's *The Creation*.[3]

---

[3] Other friends or pupils of CFH who subscribed included Queen Charlotte, the Prince of Wales, Princesses Augusta, Amelia, Elizabeth, and Mary, Edward Stephenson, and Johann Peter Salomon, the latter for 12 copies. The score of *The Creation*, including the list of subscribers, was printed in March 1800. See Landon, *Haydn: the Years of 'The Creation'*, *op. cit.*, p 482–483 and 619–632.

*c*1801	CFH and his family remove to 13 Queens Buildings, Brompton [Road], Knightsbridge.
7/8/1804	CFH's *A Collection of Divertimentos for the Piano Forte*, dedicated to HRH Princess Augusta, entered at Stationers' Hall.
1805	CEH sings in a private performance of Mozart's *Don Giovanni*, the first performance of this opera in England.
11–12/1805	CEH sings CFH's 'heroic song' *Trafalgar* to the Harmonic Society.[4]
9/12/1805	George John Horn nominated a cadet on the Madras Establishment of the East India Company.[5]
24/12/1805	CFH's published song *Trafalgar* is dedicated this day to the financier Abraham Goldsmid, as thanks for the 'many acts of friendship' he has conferred upon CFH for several years; CFH taught Goldsmid's family.
11/9/1806	CEH accompanies Charles Incledon in a performance of Incledon's *Hospitality, or The Harvest Home* at Cheltenham, where CEH meets his future wife Matilda Ray.
1/5/1807	CFH dates the preface to his arrangement 'as quartettos' of *A Sett of twelve Fugues composed for the Organ by Sebastian Bach* and dedicates this arrangement to Adolphus Frederick, Duke of Cambridge.
*c*1808	At the recommendation of Edward Stephenson, who lived at 29 Queen Square, CFH and his family remove to 25 Queen Square.
4–5/1809	CEH sings in several London concert performances of Mozart's *Don Giovanni*.

---

[4] CFH's song was composed after the Battle of Trafalgar on 21/10/1805 and before he dedicated it to Abraham Goldsmid on 24/12/1805.

[5] British Library, Oriental and India Office, cadet papers, L/MIL/9/115/65.

<5/5/1809	The first of six organ 'trios' by J. S. Bach [BWV 525–530] published in an adaptation by CFH and Samuel Wesley 'for three hands upon the piano forte'. The trios were issued singly, with the last appearing in 1811.[6]
26/6/1809	CEH makes his debut as a theatrical singer in *Up all Night, or the Smuggler's Cave* at the Lyceum Theatre, of which the music was composed by Matthew P. King.
8/4/1810	CEH takes a singing lesson from Venanzio Rauzzini in Bath. Rauzzini dies a few hours later.
30/6/1810	CEH performs at benefit for Matilda Ray at the Theatre Royal, Cheltenham.[7]
9/7/1810	*Tricks upon Travellers*, for which CEH wrote the 'serious' music and William Reeve the 'light' music, opens at the Lyceum Theatre.
19/8/1810	CEH marries Matilda Ray at Prittlewell, Essex. They make their home at [13?] Rathbone Place, London.
17/9/1810	Book I of the Samuel Wesley/CFH edition of J. S. Bach's '48' published.
26/12/1810	CEH's *The Magic Bride* opens at the Lyceum Theatre.
1–5/1811	Book II of the Samuel Wesley/CFH edition of J. S. Bach's '48' published.
19/1/1811	CEH's *The Bee Hive* opens at the Lyceum Theatre.
20/2/1811	Henrietta Horn and John Thomas Gibson marry at St George the Martyr, Queen Square.
20/5/1811	Charles Horn, son of CEH and Matilda, born. Shortly afterwards, CEH returns with his family to live at 25 Queen Square with CFH and his family.
26/8/1811	CEH's *The Boarding House, or Five Hours at Brighton* opens at the Lyceum Theatre.

---

[6] Information about the dates when these trios were published is given in Kassler and Olleson, *Samuel Wesley (1766–1837): A Source Book, op. cit.*, p 689.

[7] The bill for this performance is reproduced facing page 23.

9/9/1811	*M.P., or The Blue Stocking*, by the Irish poet Thomas Moore (1779–1852), opens at the Lyceum Theatre. CEH. who 'adapted' the music for orchestra, sings the role of Captain Canvas.[8]
9–12/1811	Book III of the Samuel Wesley/CFH edition of J. S. Bach's '48' published.
5/5/1812	Charles Horn, son of CEH and Matilda, christened at St George the Martyr, Queen Square.
6/5/1812	CEH's *The Devil's Bridge* opens at the Lyceum Theatre.
1812; >5/1812	CFH and CEH find that sharing their Queen Square home is unsuccessful. CFH and family remove to 'a smaller house' and CEH and family to a different house.
22/7/1812	*Rich and Poor*, whose overture and music were 'composed and selected' by CEH, opens at the Lyceum Theatre. CEH's selections include a fugue from J. S. Bach's '48'.
<10/10/1812	CFH ceases to be music master to TRH the princesses.
c7/1813	Book IV of the Samuel Wesley/CFH edition of J. S. Bach's '48' published.
30/10/1813	CFH's son William James Horn marries Mary Baker Strugnell.
12/4/1814	CEH's *The Woodman's Hut* opens at Drury Lane. CFH attends the first performance.
7/6/1814	CEH and Matilda Horn dine with the Hon. Charles Arbuthnot and his wife.
1/11/1814	*Jean de Paris*, with music by CEH, opens at Drury Lane.
29/11/1814	CEH's *The Ninth Statue, or The Irishman in Bagdad* opens at Drury Lane.
15/6/1815	CEH's *Charles the Bold, or The Siege of Nantz* opens at Drury Lane. A 'great deal' of the music is taken from Mozart, including 'the whole of' the *Jupiter* symphony and the slow movement from his symphony in E♭.

---

[8] *The Dramatic Censor, op. cit.*, cols. 359–366.

1/7/1816	CEH returns to the stage, performing The Seraskier in *The Siege of Belgrade* at the Lyceum Theatre.
18/12/1816	CEH performs Zemaun in the revival of *Ramah Droog; or Wine Does Wonders* at Drury Lane.
8/2/1817	Two songs by CEH in *Ramah Droog* ('If maidens would marry' and 'Turn to this heart') entered at Stationers' Hall.
17/4/1817	Thomas Attwood's *Elphi Bay, or The Arab's Faith*, in which CEH sings a song of his own composition, opens at Drury Lane.
4/6/1817	Benefit for CEH at Drury Lane. (Drury Lane playbills)
27/6/1817	CEH's song ''Tis love in the heart' from *The Election* entered at Stationers' Hall.
26/7/1817	CEH's *The Wizard, or The Brown Man of the Moor*, opens at Drury Lane.
13/8/1817	CEH's *The Persian Hunters, or The Rose of Gurgistan* opens at the Lyceum Theatre.
4/10/1817	CEH's song 'Flow flow Cubana!' from *The Persian Hunters* entered at Stationers' Hall.
4/12/1817	CFH's 'The Boatman' for three voices and piano forte, dedicated to the Duchess of Gloucester (Princess Mary), entered at Stationers' Hall.
	CEH makes his first Dublin appearance, performing in *The Devil's Bridge*.
5/6/1818	Benefit concert at the Rotunda, Dublin, for CEH and Mrs Isaac Willis, at which Michael William Balfe plays.
25/7/1818	CEH and Catherine Stephens perform in *Love in a Village* in Dublin.
22/10/1818	CEH and Catherine Stephens, after performing in Dublin and Cork, start a series of concerts in Limerick.
13/5/1820	Benefit for CEH at the Theatre Royal, Cheltenham, in which CEH performs Lord William in Stephen Storace's opera *The Haunted Tower*.[9]

---

[9] A copy of the playbill is in the Cheltenham Art Gallery and Museum.

18/7/1820	CFH's son George John Horn dies at Bangalore, India.
30/6/1824	CFH elected 'probationer' organist and master of the boys at St George's Chapel, Windsor Castle.
23/10/1824	The Drury Lane season opens with a production of Mozart's *The Marriage of Figaro* arranged by Henry Rowley Bishop, in which CEH sings the part of Fiorello. (Drury Lane playbills)
10/11/1824	First performance of Drury Lane production of Carl Maria von Weber's opera *Der Freischütz*, in which CEH sings Caspar. More than 70 performances given; the final performance is on 21/7/1825. (Drury Lane playbills)
29/11/1824	*Hafed the Gheber*, a 'new grand oriental drama', opens at Drury Lane. CEH composed 'the overture and music of the first act, with a song in the second'. (Drury Lane playbills)
4/4/1825	*Abon Hassan* opens at Drury Lane with CEH performing the title role. (Drury Lane playbills)
15/6/1825	Benefit concert for CEH at the Theatre Royal, Drury Lane, at which John Braham makes 'his first and only appearance this season in a favourite opera'.[10]
30/9/1825	CFH elected organist and master of the boys at St George's Chapel.
31/10/1826	CEH, then of 67, Judd Street, Brunswick Square, and described as a 'music and musical-instrument seller, dealer and chapman', declares himself insolvent.
10/11/1826	CEH declared bankrupt.
1/12/1826	An anonymous review of CEH's cavatina 'Cherry Ripe, sung by Madame Vestris, in *Paul Pry*' accuses CEH of copying the song from a ballad 'Let me die' by Thomas Attwood, which had been published 20 years earlier.[11]
8/1827	CEH books a passage to America.

---

[10] Advertisements on p 1 of *John Bull*, 5 and 12 June 1825.

[11] *The Harmonicon*, v 4 no. 48 (December 1826), p 245.

9/1827	CEH leaves England. His son Charles goes to Windsor Castle to stay with CFH and Diana.
1/10/1827	CEH arrives in New York City on the ship *Canada*.
17/10/1827	CEH makes his first public appearance in New York at the Park Theatre, singing The Seraskier in *The Siege of Belgrade*.
1829	CEH goes back to England.[12]
26/6/1830	George IV dies. CFH declares that his work is now done and stops writing music.
3/8/1830	CFH dies.
7/8/1830	CFH buried at St George's Chapel, Windsor.
9/8/1830	CEH granted permission to place a tablet in memory of CFH in St George's Chapel.
2/11/1830	Diana Horn granted administration of CFH's estate, valued at £450.
20/8/1831	Diana Horn buried at St George's Chapel, Windsor.
1832	CEH returns to America.[13]
27/6/1833	CEH's son Charles Horn marries Jeannette Prosser at St Nicholas Church, Brighton.
17/3/1838	CEH marries Mary Anne Horton at St James's Episcopal Church, Richmond, Virginia.[14]
12/12/1838	CEH naturalised as a US citizen by the New York City Court of Common Pleas.[15]

---

[12] A draft or copy of a letter from CEH in England to Sir George Smart dated 18 September 1829 is in the Nanki collection volume.

[13] Montague, *Charles Edward Horn, op. cit.*, p 30, places CEH in New York and Boston in November 1832.

[14] I am grateful to Gregory Stoner of the Virginia Historical Society for providing a copy of the entry of their marriage in the church register.

[15] According to Kenneth Scott, *Early New York Naturalizations: Abstracts of Naturalization Records from Federal, State and Local Courts, 1792–1840*, Baltimore, 1981, p 241. I am grateful to Peter Ray for this information.

15/3/1843	CEH comes back to London.[16]
c8/1847	In consequence of his 23/7/1847 appointment as conductor of the Handel and Haydn Society of Boston (Massachusetts) at an annual salary of $300, CEH returns to the USA.[17]
21/10/1849	CEH dies at Boston from typhoid fever,[18] intestate, leaving no known heirs in Massachusetts.[19]
11/6/1850	Commissioners appointed by the probate court find that CEH left assets of $183.99 and debts of $366.56.[20]
6/1/1887	CEH's second wife Mary Anne Horn Züst dies at Morrisania, New York.
25/4/1887	CEH's son Charles Horn dies at Hackney.

---

[16] *Musical Examiner*, 18 March 1843. I am indebted to Colin Gowing for this information.

[17] Montague, *op. cit.,* p 54–55, gives the date of CEH's appointment and salary and notes that he was in Boston in December 1847. CEH was still in London on 29/7/1847, as he wrote to Joseph Alfred Novello that day (letter at Harvard Theatre Collection).

[18] According to the register of deaths in Boston in October 1849 (v 41 p 220 no. 4601, now in the Commonwealth of Massachusetts, Office of the Secretary of State, Archives Division). I thank Peter Ray for securing a copy of this record.

[19] Suffolk County, Massachusetts, probate documents concerning the estate of CEH.

[20] *Ibid.*

INDEX OF PERSONS MENTIONED

In addition to Charles Edward Horn (CEH) and Charles Frederick Horn (CFH), the following persons are named in the texts or the accompanying notes. Persons born after 1820 have not been indexed.

a'Beckett, William (1777–1855?) 97

Abercorn, *Earl of*
see Hamilton, John James

Addison, John (1765?–1844) 41, 43

Adolphus Frederick (1774–1850), *Duke of Cambridge* 84, 114

Alexander I (1777–1825), *Tsar of Russia* 53

Alsager, Thomas Massa (1779–1846) 32

Amelia (1783–1810), *Princess* 10, 36, 113

Arbuthnot, Charles (1767–1850) 53, 116

Arbuthnot, Harriet Fane (1793–1834) 53, 116

Arne, Thomas Augustine (1710–1778) 58, 104

Arnold, Matilda Caroline (1772?–1851) 60

Arnold, Samuel James (1774–1852) 38, 43, 45, 52, 58–61

Ashe, Misses 99

Ashe, Andrew (c1759–1838) 99

Ashley, John (1734–1805) 23

Ashley-Cooper, Barbara (1788–1844) 74

Attwood, Thomas (1765–1838) 34, 64, 117–118

Augusta (1768–1840), *Princess* 10, 59–61, 84–85, 113–114

Augustus Frederick (1773–1843), *Duke of Sussex* 27

Ayrton, William (1777–1858) 1, 81, 97, 99

Babbington, Miss *or* Mrs 23, 25

Bach, Carl Philipp Emanuel (1714–1788) 96

Bach, Johann Sebastian (1685–1750) 36, 52, 55, 81, 95–96, 114–116

Bach, John Christian (1735–1782) 6

Baillie, Joanna (1762–1851) 62

Balfe, Michael William (1808–1870) 68, 74, 117

Barham, Thomas Foster (1766–1844) 96

Barthelemon *later* Henslowe, Cecilia Maria (bc1770) 34, 112

Baumgarten, Charles Frederick (c1738–1824) 87

Beaufort, *Duchess of*
see Leveson-Gower, Charlotte Sophia

Beaufort, *Duke of*
see Somerset, Henry Charles Fitzroy

Beazley, Samuel (1786–1851) 48–49, 55

Bedford, Paul (1792?–1841) 70

Beethoven, Ludwig van (bap1770–1827) 19

Bellamy, Thomas Ludford (1771–
1843) 33
Bertram, Charles 3–4, 34
Bickerstaffe, Isaac (1735–1812)
62
Billington, Elizabeth (*d*1818) 30,
32, 37, 78, 88
Bishop, Elizabeth Sarah
see Lyon, Elizabeth Sarah
Bishop, *Sir* Henry Rowley (1768–
1855) 37–39, 44–45, 55–57, 68,
108, 118
Bland, John (*c*1750–*c*1840) 13,
113
Bland, Maria Theresa (1770–1838)
14, 30, 63
Blizard, Jane 36
Blizard, *Sir* William (1743–1835)
36
Blizard, *Lady* 36
Blomberg, *Rev.* Frederick William
(1761–1847) 85
Blücher von Wahlstatt, *Marshal*
Gebhard Leberecht (1742–1819)
53
Bochsa, Nicholas (1789–1856) 99
Boildieu, François Adrien (1775–
1834) 54
Bolton, Eliza 50
Bolton, Mary Catherine, *Lady*
Thurlow (*c*1790–1830) 50
Bonaparte, Napoléon (1769–1821),
Emperor of France 53
Bosville, Godfrey *see* Macdonald,
Godfrey Bosville
Bown, James *see* Winston, James
Braham, John (1777–1856) 27,
29–30, 37, 50–52, 61, 78, 88, 118
Bridgetower, Frederick Augustus
15
Bridgetower, George Polgreen
(1778–1860) 15
Broadhurst, Mr 64

Broadwood, John (1732–1812) 24
Broderip, Francis Fane (*d*1807)
2–4
Brühl, *Count* John Maurice von *or*
Hans Moritz von (1736–1809)
73, 82
Buggins, Lavinia *or* Louisa
see Hammersley, Lavinia
Buggins, Miriam H.
see Hammersley, Miriam
Buggins, Samuel 63
Bunn, Alfred (1796–1860) 106
Burdett, *Sir* Francis (1770–1844)
31
Burges, *Sir* James Bland, *later*
Sir James Lamb (1752–1824) 49
Burney, Charles (1726–1814) 26
Byrn, Oscar (*c*1795–1867) 38
Byrne, Mary 65

Caigniez, Louis-Charles (1762–
1842) 56–57
Cambridge, *Duke of*
see Adolphus Frederick
Capell, George, *5th Earl of Essex*
57
Carlisle, *Earl*
see Howard, Frederick
Carr, Miss 100
Cecil, James (1748–1823), *7th*
Earl of Salisbury, 1st Marquess
of Salisbury, Lord Chamberlain
20
Charlotte (1744–1818), *Queen* 2,
6–7, 20–21, 53, 59–61, 70, 74,
83–84, 87, 89–90, 112–113
Charlotte (1766–1828),
Princess Royal 10
Cheese, Miss
see Willis, Mrs Isaac
Cist, Lewis J. (1818–1885) 109
Clementi, Muzio (1752–1832) 3,
6, 73–74, 83

Cobb, James (1756–1818) 62
Coffey, Charles (*d*1745) 100
Cohen, Misses 23–24
Cohen, Hymen 23–25
Coleraine, *Baron*
  see Hanger, George
Cooke, George Frederick (1756–
  1812) 29
Cooke, William 36
Copley, John Singleton *the elder*
  (1737–1815) 31
Corelli, Arcangelo (1653–1713)
  15
Corri, Domenico (1746–1825) 23,
  34
Coveney, Mr 62
Cowell, Mr 96
Crosdill, John (*c*1751–1825) 17

Dahmen, Johann Arnold (*bc*1760)
  32
Davenport, Mary Ann (1759–1843)
  30
Davy, John (1763–1824) 68
D'Egville, James Harvey (*c*1770–
  >1835) 38
Delavaux, Francis Hugh Adean 10
Dibdin, Thomas John (1771–1841)
  56, 77, 104
Dickons, Martha 'Maria' Poole
  (1774–1833) 52
Dignum, Charles (*c*1765–1827) 14
Dowton, William (1764–1851) 29,
  38, 40
Doyle, Mr 38
Dragonetti, Domenico (1794–
  1846) 15, 32
Duffy, Mr 102
Dupont, Diana Arboneau
  see Horn, Diana
Dupont, Elizabeth (CFH's mother-
  in-law) 5

Dupont, Frederick John (CFH's
  brother-in-law, *bap*1765) 6
Dupont, John (CFH's brother-in-
  law) 6, 27
Dupont, John Arboneau (CFH's
  father-in-law, *dc*1806) 5, 20, 27
Dussek, Jan Ladislav (1760–1812)
  22

Edwin, Elizabeth Rebecca (*d*1854)
  45
Elizabeth (1770–1840), *Princess*
  10, 113
Elliston, Robert William (1774–
  1831) 56, 63–64, 97–100, 103–
  104, 107–108
Emery, John (1777–1822) 30
Essex, *Countess of*
  see Stephens, Catherine
Essex, *Earl of see* Capell, George

Fane, Harriet
  see Arbuthnot, Harriet Fane
Farren, William (1786–1861) 66,
  68
Fawcett Jr, John (1768–1837) 30,
  52
Feron, Elisabeth 33
Fischer, Johann Christian *or*
  John Christian (1733–1800) 11
Fitzgerald, Maurice 66
Fitzgerald, William Vesey (*c*1782–
  1843), *Baron Fitzgerald and
  Vesey* 66–68
Forkel, Johann Nicholas (1749–
  1818) 37
Frederick William III (1770–1840),
  King of Prussia 53

Garlick, Thomas 74
Garrick, David (1717–1779) 30–
  31

Garrick, Eva Maria (1724–1822)
30–31
Gatti, Madame
see Hughes, Maria
Gelinek, Josef (1758–1825) 19
George III (1738–1820), *King*
7, 20–21, 36, 38, 59–60, 70, 83–
84
George IV (1762–1830), *King,
earlier Prince of Wales and
Prince Regent* 32, 53, 83, 85,
113, 119
German-Reed, Priscilla
see Horton, Priscilla
German-Reed, Thomas
(1817–1888) 29
Gibbs, *Lady* Frances (*d*1843) 25
Gibbs, *Sir* Vicary (1751–1820) 25
Gibson, *Rev.* Charles Dockley
(1818–1869) 22
Gibson, Bowes John (*bap*1744) 25
Gibson, George 21, 25
Gibson, George Collins 28
Gibson, John Thomas (CEH's
brother-in-law, 1785–1851)
21–22, 25, 49, 115
Giornovichi, Giovanni Mane
(*d*1804) 19
Glossop, Elisabeth
see Feron, Elisabeth
Glossop, Joseph 33
Gloucester, *Duchess of*
see Mary, *Princess*
Gloucester, *Duke of*
see William Frederick
Goldsmid, Abraham (1756?–1810)
24, 95, 114
Goodall, Mr 17
Goodwin, Thomas (1799–1886)
104–105
Gower, *Earl of*
see Leveson-Gower, Granville

Gower, *Lady*
see Leveson-Gower, Susanna
Graham, *Col.* 35
Graham, Misses 26
Green, Valentine (1739–1831) 31
Griffin Jr, George Eugene (1781–
1863) 32
Griglietti, Elizabeth Augusta 33
Guilford, *Earl of*
see North, Frederick

Hässler, Johann Wilhelm (1747–
1822) 112
Hamilton, John James (1756–
1818), *9th Earl of Abercorn* 26,
35
Hammersley, Lavinia 63
Hammersley, Miriam 63–64, 98
Handel, George Frideric (1685–
1759) 16, 20–21, 58
Hanger, George (1751?–1824), *4th
Baron Coleraine of the 2nd
creation* 53–54
Harley, John Pritt (1786–1858)
101, 103
Harrison, Samuel (1760?–1812)
20–21
Hartman, Carl 16–17
Hawes, William (1785–1846) 57,
96
Haydn, Joseph (1732–1809) 13–
15, 34, 45, 87–88, 112–113
Hayward, Thomas 33, 50
Heavy, Mr 48
Heinrich, Anthony Philip (1781–
1861) 106
Hemans, Felicia (1793–1835) 109
Henslowe, Cecilia Maria
see Barthelemon, Cecilia Maria
Herschel, *Sir* William (1738–1822)
60
Hill, Henry (1781–1839) 98

Hobart, *Rev.* Henry Lewis (1774–1846) 86, 105

Hook, Theodore Edward (1788–1841) 31

Horn, Charles (CEH's and Matilda Horn's son, 1811–1887) 48–51, 70–71, 91, 97, 101, 103, 115–116, 119–120

Horn, Diana [*née* Dupont] (CFH's wife, 1764–1831) 5–7, 10–12, 47–48, 50, 82, 91, 109, 111, 119

Horn, Ferdinand (not related to CFH) 2

Horn, Frederick Thomas (CEH's brother, *b*1787) 9–10, 15, 18–20, 86, 112

Horn, George John (*b*1790, CEH's brother) 17–18, 83, 86, 112, 114, 118

Horn, Henrietta Elizabeth (CEH's sister, *bap*1789) 10, 18, 21–22, 47, 49, 112, 115

Horn, J. Christian *or* J. Christopher (CFH's brother) 1

Horn, Jane (CFH's sister) 1, 86

Horn, Jeannette [*née* Prosser] (CEH's daughter-in-law) 70, 91, 103, 119

Horn, John Wolfgang (CFH's father, *b*1737) 1

Horn, Louisa Maria (CEH's sister, *b*1794) 18, 90, 113

Horn, Mary *or* Maria (CFH's sister) 1, 10, 19, 33–34, 86, 112

Horn, Mary Anne [*née* Horton] (CEH's second wife, 1811–1887) 28, 95, 103, 119–120

Horn, Mary Baker [*née* Strugnell] (CEH's sister-in-law) 116

Horn, Matilda [*née* Ray] (CEH's first wife, *b*1792) 28, 46–48, 51, 63, 95, 97, 99, 104, 107–108, 114–115

Horn *later* Sewell, Sophia (CEH's sister, *b*1797) 18, 90, 113

Horn, Sophia Dorothea (CFH's mother, 1735–1798) 1, 10, 19–20, 86, 112–113

Horn, William James (CEH's brother, *b*1792) 18, 74, 86, 113, 116

Horton, Mary Anne
see Horn, Mary Anne

Horton *later* German-Reed, Priscilla (Mary Anne Horn's sister, 1818–1895) 29

Horton, Mr (Mary Anne Horn's brother) 109

Howard, Bernard Edward, *12th Duke of Norfolk* (1765–1842) 50

Howard, Frederick, *5th Earl of Carlisle* (1748–1825) 5

Howard, Henry Charles, *13th Duke of Norfolk* (1791–1856) 50

Howard, Margaret Caroline, *Lady Carlisle see* Leveson-Gower, Margaret Caroline

Hughes, Elizabeth 102

Hughes, Maria (*b*1789) 33

Hunt, Henry 58

Hunt, Lydia Ellen
see Merry, Lydia Ellen

Incledon, Charles (1763–1826) 27–28, 30, 37, 46, 48, 77–78, 114

Jeudwine, Thomas 53–54

Johnstone, John Henry (1749–1828) 30, 42, 48, 54–55, 62

Jones, Frederick Edward (*c*1759–1834) 65–67

Jones, John (1796–1861) 64–65

Jordan, Dora (1761–1861) 29

Kelly, Frances Maria (1790–1882) 38, 46, 52, 58

Kelly, Lydia Eliza (*b*1795) 58, 65
Kelly, Michael (*c*1762–1826) 11,
    30, 38, 43, 65
Kemble, Charles (1775–1854) 29,
    96
Kemble, John Philip (1757–1823)
    29
Kilsby, Martha
    see Rowlett, Martha
King, Mr 1
King, Julia 74
King, Maria 74
King, Matthew Peter (1773?–1823)
    38, 43, 88, 115
Kollmann, Augustus Frederic
    Christopher (1756–1829) 36
Koželuch, Leopold (1747–1818)
    13–14, 113

Laing, David 22
Laing, *Rev.* Henry (*bap*1784–
    *c*1872) 21–22
Laing, John (*bap*1785) 21–22
Laing, Louisa (1816–1903) 22
Laing, Thomas (*bap*1773) 22
Lamb, Charles 107
Lamb, *Sir* James
    see Burges, *Sir* James Bland
Langdon, Mr and Mrs 53
Lazenby, Elizabeth
    see Griglietti, Elizabeth Augusta
Lazenby, George 33
Lee, Louis Leoni (*d*>1862) 64
Leveson-Gower, Charlotte (1788–
    1870), *Duchess of Norfolk* 50
Leveson-Gower, Charlotte Sophia
    (1771–1854), *Duchess of
    Beaufort* 4, 7, 73, 82, 111
Leveson-Gower, Georgiana
    Augusta (1769–1806) 4, 73, 111
Leveson-Gower, Granville (1721–
    1803), *2nd Earl Gower,*

1st Marquis of Stafford 4, 6, 50,
    73, 82
Leveson-Gower, Margaret Caroline
    (1753–1824), *Lady Carlisle* 4
Leveson-Gower, Susanna [*née*
    Stewart] (1743–1805), *Lady
    Gower, Marchioness of Stafford*
    4, 82
Lewis, Matthew Gregory
    (1775–1818) 40, 43–44, 52, 55
Lewis, William Thomas (*d*1811)
    30
Lindley, Robert (1776–1855) 32
Longman, John 2
Loudoun, Countess of
    see Mure-Campbell, Flora
Louis XVI (1754–1793),
    King of France 18
Lovegrove, William (1778–1816)
    46
Luppino *later* Noble, Georgina *or*
    Rosina (1778–1832) 38, 41
Lyon *later* Bishop, Elizabeth Sarah
    (1787–1831) 29, 37, 40
Lyttleton, Thomas (1744–1779),
    2nd Baron Lyttleton 54

McCaskey, James 37, 65
Macdonald, Angus 25
Macdonald, Godfrey Bosville,
    3rd Baron Macdonald of Sleat
    (1775–1832) 25–26
Macdonald, Mrs 25
Macfarren, John (1818–1901) 103
Mackay, Charles (1814–1889) 107
Mackenzie, Frances Cerjat
    see Gibbs, *Lady* Frances
Mackenzie, Robert Shelton (1809–
    1881) 103, 107
Mackinlay, Thomas 102, 106
Macleod, Charlotte Carolina
    (*b*1799) 49

Macleod *later* Mure-Campbell,
Flora (*c*1764–1780) 35
Macleod, Georgiana Tweedale
(1798–1818) 49
Macleod 'of Colbecks', Jane (*or
Jean*) 35, 49
Macleod 'of Colbecks', *Col.* John
(*d*1823) 35, 49
Mangeon, Elizabeth 62
Mangeon, Harriet (1796–1863) 62
Mangeon, Henrietta Charlotte Lucy
(*b*1798) 62
Mangeon, William (*c*1772–1816)
62
Marshall, Thomas (*d*1819?) 44
Mary (1776–1857), *Princess, later
Duchess of Gloucester* 10, 36,
85, 113, 117
Mason, Charles 109
Mathews, Anne Jackson (*c*1782–
1869) 42
Mathews, Charles (1776–1835)
41–42, 46, 48, 77
Mathews, Charles James (1803–
1878) 42–43
Mathews, Lucia Elizabetta
Bartolozzi Vestris (1797–1856)
42, 103, 118
Mazzinghi, Joseph 62
Merry *later* Hunt, Lydia Ellen 58,
61–63
Millingen, John Gideon (1782–
1862) 56
Millington, Mr 99
Mizler von Kolof, Lorenz (1711–
1778) 81
Moira, *Earl of*
see Rawdon-Hastings, Francis
Moira, *Lady*
see Mure-Campbell, Flora
Moncrieff, William Thomas
(1794–1857) 101

Monzani, Emily
see Prosser, Emily
Monzani, Tebaldo (1762–1839) 70
Monzani, Theobald Peregrine
(*bap*1811) 70
Moore, Thomas (1779–1852) 116
Mori, Nicholas 98
Morris, *Col. later Gen.* George
Pope (1802–1864) 98, 103, 107
Mountain, John (*b*1766) 42
Mountain, Sarah (1768–1841) 14,
30, 37–38, 40, 42, 45–46, 48
Mountain, William J. 37–38
Mozart, Wolfgang Amadeus
(1756–1791) 11, 16, 32–34, 45,
50–51, 56, 64, 101, 113–114,
116, 118
Munden, Joseph Shepherd (1758–
1832) 47–48, 62, 99
Mure-Campbell, Flora (*c*1764–
1780) *see* Macleod *later*
Mure-Campbell, Flora
Mure-Campbell, Flora, *Countess of
Loudoun, Lady Moira*
(1780–1840) 35–36
Mure-Campbell, James,
5th Earl of Loudoun (1726–
1786) 35
Musgrove [Musgrave?], Mr 32

Nairne, Charles 13
Naldi, Guiseppe (1770–1820) 25,
33
Neate, Charles (1784–1877) 17–
19, 22–23
Nelson, *Admiral* Horatio (1758–
1805) 27
Noble, Georgina *or* Rosina
see Luppino, Georgina
Noble, Henry 41
Norfolk, *12th Duke of*
see Howard, Bernard Edward

Norfolk, *13th Duke of*
  see Howard, Henry Charles
North, Frederick (1732–1792), *2nd Earl of Guilford, Prime Minister*
  5–6
Novello, Joseph Alfred (1810–1896) 102, 120
Novello, Vincent (1781–1861) 96

Orger, Mary Ann (1788–1849) 38

Page, Elizabeth
  see Dupont, Elizabeth
Page, *Rev.* John (c1760–1812) 10–11, 16
Papendiek, Charlotte (1765–1839) 7, 10, 112
Pasta, Giuditta (1797–1865) 98
Peake, Richard (1757–1829) 61
Pearman, William (b1792) 65
Phillips, Henry (1801–1876) 106
Phillips, Thomas (1774–1841) 37–38, 40, 42–43, 48
Pindar, Peter *pseudonym*
  see Wolcot, John
Pinnock, William (1782–1843) 74
Pinto, George Frederick (1785–1806) 18
Pitt, William (1759–1806), *Prime Minister* 7
Planché, James Robinson (1796–1880) 107
Pleyel, Ignace Joseph (1757–1831) 17
Pocock, Isaac (1782–1835) 50, 68
Ponsonby, *Lady* Frances Anne Georgiana (1817–1910) 74
Ponsonby, William Francis Spencer (1787–1855) 74
Porter, William Trotter (1809–1858) 101
Powell, William (1762–1812) 40
Power, James (1766–1836) 52

Price, Stephen (d1840) 69
Prosser, Emily (bc1812) 70
Prosser, Jeannette
  see Horn, Jeannette
Pucitta, Vincenzo (1778–1861) 34
Purday, Charles Henry (1799–1885) 32–33, 87
Pye, Matilda Caroline
  see Arnold, Matilda Caroline
Pyne, James Kendrick (1785–1857) 44

Quick, John (1748–1851) 41

Rae, Alexander (1782–1820) 107
Ramsbottom, John Sr 12
Ramsbottom, John Jr (c1780–1845) 12
Ramsbottom, Richard (c1749–1813) 12
Rauzzini, Venanzio (c1746–1810) 36–37, 78, 115
Rawdon-Hastings, Flora
  see Mure-Campbell, Flora
Rawdon-Hastings, Francis, *2nd Earl of Moira* 35
Ray, Mr (Matilda Horn's brother) 104
Ray, Alfred Gustavus (Matilda Horn's nephew, bap1811) 70
Ray, Edward Adam (Matilda Horn's father, bap1766) 28, 47, 50
Ray, Harriott (Matilda Horn's sister, bap1789) 47–48
Ray, Matilda
  see Horn, Matilda
Reed, Priscilla
  see Horton, Priscilla
Reed, Thomas German
  see German-Reed, Thomas
Reeve, William (1757–1815) 29, 49, 62, 115

Richardson, Misses 26
Ries, Ferdinand (1784–1838) 62
Ries, Harriet
    see Mangeon, Harriet
Roberts, Mr 26
Robins, George Henry (1748–
    1851) 41, 64, 69, 98, 104
Rogers, *Captain* James 70
Roper, W. J. 42–43
Rossini, Gioachino (1792–1868)
    56
Rovedino, Carlo (1751–1822) 52
Rovedino, Tommasso (1789–1860)
    52
Rowlatt, Mr 50
Rowlatt, Mrs 50–51
Rowlett, Martha 50
Rowlett, William 50
Russell, Henry (1812–1900) 101
Russell, Samuel Thomas (*c*1770–
    1845) 102

Sainsbury, John Davis (*bc*1793) 73
St Croix, William de (1787–1843)
    105
Salieri, Antonio (1750–1825) 19
Salisbury, *Earl of* and *Marquess of*
    see Cecil, James
Salomon, John Peter *or* Johann
    Peter (1745–1815) 6, 9, 15, 31,
    112–113
Schick, Anthony *or* Anton 24
Schröter, Christoph Gottlieb
    (1699–1782) 81, 111
Schwindl, Frederick (1737–1786)
    15
Scott, *Sir* Walter (1771–1832) 64
Sewell, Daniel (CEH's brother-in-
    law) 90
Sewell, George (CFH's grandson)
    90
Sewell, Sophia *see* Horn, Sophia
Sexton, William (1764–1824) 85

Shakespeare, William (1564–1616)
    29, 41
Sharp, Benjamin (1784–1875) 34
Shenaman, Sophia Dorothea
    see Horn, Sophia Dorothea
Sheridan, Richard Brinsley (1751–
    1816) 41, 44
Shirreff, Jane (1811–1883) 57
Siboni, Giuseppe (1780–1839) 33
Siddons, Sarah Kemble (1775–
    1831) 29, 61
Simpson, Mr and Mrs 49
Simpson, Edmund Shaw (1784–
    1848) 69, 105
Sinclair, John (1790–1857) 57
Skeffington, *Sir* Lumley St George
    (1771–1850) 45, 55
Smart, *Sir* George (1776–1867)
    38, 50, 96
Smart, Henry (1778–1823) 38, 57,
    64
Smith, Miss (*later* Mrs Byrn) 38
Smith, George (*b*1777) 38, 40
Smith, Horatio (1779–1849) 46
Smith, James (1775–1839) 46
Smith, John (1797–1861) 65
Smith, Thomas 14
Soane, *Sir* John (1753–1837)
    26–27
Somerset, Henry Charles Fitzroy
    (1766–1835), *6th Duke of*
    Beaufort 4, 73
Sophia (1777–1848), *Princess* 36
Spray, John (*d*1827) 65
Stafford, *Marchioness of*
    see Leveson-Gower, Susanna
Stafford, *Marquis of*
    see Leveson-Gower, Granville
Stapleton, Mr 67, 97
Stenson, *Major* 50
Stephens, Catherine,
    Countess of Essex (1794–1882)
    57, 68–69, 103, 117

Stephenson, Edward (1759–1833)
    9, 25, 37, 50, 97, 112–114
Stephenson, Rowland (1782–1856)
    97
Sterland, John (*c*1769–1854) 24
Stevenson, *Sir* John (1761–1833)
    65
Stewart, Susanna
    see Leveson-Gower, Susanna
Storace, Anna Selina 'Nancy'
    (1765–1817) 29–30, 37, 50, 78
Storace, Stephen (1762–1796) 29,
    58, 65, 117
Strugnell, Mary Baker
    see Horn, Mary Baker
Sussex, *Duke of*
    see Augustus Frederick

Taylor, Edward (1784–1863) 97
Taylor, *General Sir* Herbert (1775–
    1839) 60
Thomson, Mr H. 48
Thurlow *later* Hovell-Thurlow,
    Edward, *2nd Baron Thurlow*
    (1781–1829) 50
Thurlow, *Lady*
    see Bolton, Mary Catherine

Vesey Fitzgerald, William
    see Fitzgerald, William Vesey
Vestris, Madame
    see Mathews, Lucia Elizabetta
    Bartolozzi Vestris
von Zinge, Mr *see* Zinge, Mr von

Waldegrave, *Lady* Caroline (1765–
    1831) 73–74, 82–83
Wallack, James William (1795–
    1864) 56, 101
Ware, William Henry (1777–1828)
    15
Watson, *Sir* Brook (1724–1822)
    30–31

Watson, Helen 31
Weber, Carl Maria von (1786–
    1826) 70, 118
Webster, Benjamin Nottingham
    (1797–1882) 102
Webster, Mr J. 106
Wellington, *Duke of see*
    Wesley *later* Wellesley, Arthur
Welsh, Mary Anne
    see Wilson, Mary Anne
Welsh, Thomas (1770–1848) 57–
    62, 88, 97, 107
Wemyss, Francis Courtney (1797–
    1859) 100–101
Wesley *later* Wellesley, Arthur
    (1769–1852), *Duke of Wellington*
    53
Wesley, Samuel (1766–1837) 18,
    26, 84, 95, 115–116
Wetenhall, Ann (*bap*1777) 13–14,
    88, 113
Wetenhall, Betty 14
Wetenhall, Edward 13–15, 18, 113
Wetenhall [Jr], Edward (*bap*1779)
    14–15
William IV (1765–1837), *King*
    89–90
William Frederick, *2nd Duke of*
    Gloucester of the Georgian
    creation (1776–1854) 35–36
Williams, Thomas 99
Willis, Mrs Isaac 68, 117
Wilson, *Lt Col.* John (*d*1812) 26,
    34–35
Wilson, Mary Anne (1802–1867)
    57, 107
Windsor, James W. (1776–1853)
    17
Winkelman, Mr 2
Winston, James (1774–1843) 28,
    69, 98, 100, 103, 108
Winter, Peter von (1754–1825) 32,
    34

Wolcot, John (1738–1819) 70

Zinge, Mr von 1

Züst, Mr 28
Züst, Mary Anne
  see Horn, Mary Anne